NEWMAN AND THE FULLNESS OF CHRISTIANITY

Ian Ker

T&T CLARK
EDINBURGH

T&T CLARK LTD
59 GEORGE STREET
EDINBURGH EH2 2LQ
SCOTLAND

First published 1993
Latest impression 1998

ISBN 0 567 29225 8

British Library Cataloguing-in-Publication Data
A catalogue record for this book is available from the British Library

Typeset by Buccleuch Printers Ltd, Hawick
Printed and in Great Britain by MPG Books Ltd, Bodmin

Contents

Acknowledgements

The substance of this book was given as the 1992 Fisher Lectures at Cambridge University.

For the honour of being invited to contribute to this distinguished series of lectures and for an abundance of hospitality I am very grateful to the Revd. John Osman, the Catholic Chaplain.

Stratford Caldecott suggested that I should publish the lectures in an expanded form, and I am indebted to him for his comments on the typescript.

I must also thank two other friends, the Revd. James Reidy and the Revd. Michael Barber, SJ, for their encouragement and help.

I express, too, my thanks to Sue Butt for her heroic patience in typing an indecipherable manuscript.

Abbreviations

Newman collected his works in a uniform edition of 36 vols. (1868–81). Until his death in 1890 he continued making minor textual changes in reprints of individual volumes in this edition, of which all the volumes from 1886 were published by Longmans, Green & Co. of London. References are usually to volumes in the uniform edition published after 1890 by Longmans, which are distinguished from other editions by not including details in parentheses after the title.

Apo.	*Apologia pro Vita Sua*, ed. Martin J. Svaglic (Oxford: Clarendon Press, 1967)
Ari.	*The Arians of the Fourth Century*
Ath. i, ii	*Select Treatises of St. Athanasius*, 2 vols.
AW	*John Henry Newman: Autobiographical Writings*, ed. Henry Tristram (London and New York: Sheed & Ward, 1956)
Call.	*Callista: A Tale of the Third Century*
Campaign	*My Campaign in Ireland, Part I*, ed. W. Neville (privately printed, 1896)
Cons.	*On Consulting the Faithful in Matters of Doctrine*, ed. John Coulson (London: Geoffrey Chapman, 1961)
DA	*Discussions and Arguments on Various Subjects*
Dev.	*An Essay on the Development of Christian Doctrine*
Diff. i, ii	*Certain Difficulties felt by Anglicans in Catholic Teaching*, 2 vols.

Ess. i, ii	*Essays Critical and Historical,* 2 vols.
GA	*An Essay in Aid of a Grammar of Assent,* ed. I. T. Ker (Oxford: Clarendon Press, 1985)
HS i, ii, iii	*Historical Sketches,* 3 vols.
Idea	*The Idea of a University,* ed. I. T. Ker (Oxford: Clarendon Press, 1976)
Jfc.	*Lectures on the Doctrine of Justification*
LD i-vi, xi-xxxi	*The Letters and Diaries of John Henry Newman,* ed. Charles Stephen Dessain *et al.,* vols. i-vi (Oxford: Clarendon Press, 1978–84), xi-xxii (London: Nelson, 1961–72), xxiii-xxxi (Oxford: Clarendon Press, 1973–77)
LG	*Loss and Gain: The Story of a Convert*
Mix.	*Discourses addressed to Mixed Congregations*
NO	*Newman the Oratorian: His unpublished Oratory Papers,* ed. Placid Murray, OSB (Dublin: Gill & Macmillan, 1969)
OS	*Sermons preached on Various Occasions*
PS i-viii	*Parochial and Plain Sermons,* 8 vols.
Phil.N. i, ii	*The Philosophical Notebook of John Henry Newman,* ed. Edward Sillem, 2 vols. (Louvain: Nauwelaerts, 1969–70)
Prepos.	*Present Position of Catholics in England*
SD	*Sermons bearing on Subjects of the Day*
TT	*Tracts Theological and Ecclesiastical*
US	*Fifteen Sermons preached before the University of Oxford*
VM i, ii	*The Via Media,* 2 vols.
VV	*Verses on Various Occasions*
Ker	Ian Ker, *John Henry Newman: A Biography* (Oxford: Clarendon Press, 1988)

I

The Varieties of Christianity

Pope John Paul II has called for the re-evangelisation of Europe during the 1990s. On 22 January 1991 the Pope declared John Henry Cardinal Newman (1801–90) to be 'Venerable', the first formal step towards his canonisation. The proximity of the two events may be more providential than coincidental. Many believe that not only will Newman be eventually canonised but that this will be accompanied by the recognition that he is a 'Doctor of the Church', that is, a teacher whose writings carry a special authority qualitatively different from and superior to that of the most brilliant and learned theologians. Just as St. Thomas Aquinas was the great Doctor of the middle ages and St. Robert Bellarmine of the Counter-Reformation, so Newman may come to be seen as the Doctor of the new era in the Church's history which was initiated by the Second Vatican Council (1962–5). Newman has indeed often been called the 'Father of Vatican II', because he more than any other comparable figure anticipated and predicted the reforms of that Council; but, if that is so, then it must also be true that he carries particular weight for the interpretation and development of the conciliar teachings, a process which can only be said to have begun. There is another way too in which Newman may be said to be a prophet for our times, and that is in his frequent sombre predictions of modern secularisation, a phenomenon that was already clearly recognisable in his own day.

From both these points of view Newman's name deserves to be closely linked with the pressing need to re-evangelise the post-Christian culture of Western society. This consumer materialism is now threatening the countries of Eastern Europe and the Soviet Union, whose liberation from Communist materialism began in 1990. The attempt to restore the spiritual dimension to a new re-united Europe has obvious ecumenical implications. And here again Newman's life and work have a particular significance. Just as the work of the Second Vatican Council was intended not only to introduce a renewal into the life of the Catholic Church but also at the same time to encourage the movement towards Christian unity, so too Newman saw that the reforms in Catholicism he advocated were essential if there was to be any hope of a rapprochement between Rome and other Christians.

Newman once wrote that 'the Church must be prepared for converts'.[1] This was at a time when, under the predominant influence of Ultramontanism, the Catholic Church seemed intent on ever more obscurantist and reactionary policies. But he never despaired of far-reaching changes eventually, and thought there was more hope of the Catholic Church becoming more 'Christian' than of the Church of England becoming more 'Catholic'. This seems prophetic when one considers on the one hand the extent to which the Catholic Church has changed since Vatican II, and on the other hand the way in which Anglo-Catholicism has so sharply declined in England since its peak in the 1930s.[2] And while there have been many changes in externals which suggest an increasingly Catholic Church of England, on the other hand the continual erosion of doctrine and the readiness to make fundamental changes to the sacrament of holy orders support Newman's fear that the Anglican Church might become so 'radically liberalised . . . as to become a simple enemy of the Truth'.[3] When, too, one considers the secularising activities of the World Council of Churches and the widespread collapse of doctrinal orthodoxy in Protestantism, one can see that Newman's remark has a much wider significance.

Newman had early on as an Anglican predicted the 'great attack upon the Bible' which gathered force during the nineteenth century.[4] He saw that the use of Biblical criticism,

---

[1] *AW* 258.
[2] See W. S. F. Pickering, *Anglo-Catholicism: A Study in Religious Ambiguity* (London: Routledge, 1989).
[3] *LD* xxi. 299.
[4] See *Ker* 193.

together with scientific discoveries which undermined the literal truth of the Scriptures, would between them sound the death-knell for Protestantism. By substituting the Bible for the Church at the Reformation, Protestants would be left without any final authority in matters of faith. Whereas the literal truth of the Bible was not 'one of life and death' to a Catholic, 'we are witnessing the beginning of the end of Protestantism, the breaking of that bubble of "Bible-Christianity" which has been its life'.[5] When one looks today at the Protestant parts of Europe – Britain, Scandinavia, northern Germany, where church attendance has reached a remarkably uniform level of about two per cent – at least five times worse than France, the most de-Christianised country in Catholic Europe – one can see the truth of Newman's observation that 'a book, after all, cannot make a stand against the wild living intellect of man'.[6]

It is a remarkable fact, which has surprisingly gone unnoticed, that in his own life Newman experienced to different degrees all the main varieties of Christianity. In this sense alone he is a figure of considerable ecumenical interest. Before turning to the specific ways in which he can contribute to contemporary evangelisation, it will be useful to examine the extent to which his final view of Christianity represents a fusion of what he saw as the positive elements of the main Christian traditions, and how far his criticisms of the negative features helped to constitute the eventual synthesis he looked for in a reformed and renewed Catholicism.

Newman grew up as an ordinary member of the established Church of England. His parents belonged to what their son was later to call 'the national religion of England' or 'Bible Religion', consisting 'not in rites or creeds, but mainly in having the Bible read in Church, in the family, and in private'.[7] He himself was 'brought up from a child to take great delight in reading the Bible'.[8] His earliest religious experience, then, was of the kind of Biblical Protestantism which was once so widespread in England and other European countries and which has survived much

[5] *LD* xx. 465.
[6] *Apo.* 219.
[7] *GA* 43.
[8] See *Ker* 3.

better in the United States of America, although it is now rapidly declining there too. It is a religion, as Newman foresaw, that would hardly survive the chill winds of secularism and unbelief. So essentially undogmatic is it in practice, if not theory, that Newman could say that he had 'no formed religious convictions' till he was 15.[9]

It was in the summer of 1816 that he underwent an Evangelical-style conversion under the influence of one of his schoolmasters, who had himself only shortly before – but after taking holy orders in the Church of England – became a born-again Christian, as we should now say. The Wesleyan revival was still in full flood and only a few years later the novelist George Eliot was herself to undergo a similar conversion at the same age and also under the influence of a school teacher. Like so many other Victorians, both came to reject the tenets of the Evangelicalism that had so powerfully affected them in adolescence, but in both cases the formative influence was lasting. It is true that Newman soon became aware that he had not apparently undergone the full emotional experience of 'the Evangelical process of conversion' with 'its stages of conviction of sin, terror, despair, news of the free and full salvation, joy and peace, and so on to final perseverance', for his feelings had not been *'violent'* in the required manner, 'but a returning to, a renewing of, principles, under the power of the Holy Spirit, which I had *already* felt, and in a measure acted on, when young'. But even if he had not had 'those special Evangelical experiences, which, like the grip of the hand or other prescribed signs of a secret society, are the true token of a member', still it was close enough to such a conversion to deceive all but the most doctrinaire, and there was certainly no doubting the Calvinist doctrines which he now accepted as part and parcel of the Christian faith. Last but not least, he now knew for himself the 'reality of conversion'.[10]

Newman's election to a fellowship at Oriel College, Oxford in 1822 brought him into close contact with the leading Anglican Latitudinarians or liberals of the age. By the end of 1827 he was

---

[9] *Apo.* 15.
[10] *AW* 80, 150, 172.

'drifting in the direction of the Liberalism of the day'.[11] A particularly important influence was the logician Richard Whately (1787–1863). In his autobiographical memoir Newman contrasts his influence with that of the Regius Professor of Divinity, Charles Lloyd (1784–1829), whose (private) theology class, which Newman attended, on the Catholic and medieval sources of the Anglican Book of Common Prayer anticipated the teachings of the Tractarians. Whereas Whately's 'great satisfaction was to find a layman who had made a creed for himself' and felt sympathy for 'a heretic, for his heresy at least showed that he had exercised his mind upon its subject matter', Lloyd, who was a 'scholar' not an 'original thinker', stressed doctrine and tradition. But while there was no doubting who was 'more Catholic in his tone of mind', it was the free-thinking Whately who exerted the real 'intellectual influence' on Newman by teaching him how to think for himself.[12]

In the same year of his conversion, 1816, Newman had read Joseph Milner's five-volume *Church History* (1794–1809) and was 'nothing short of enamoured of the long extracts' from the Fathers.[13] The 'permanent effect' of this reading was that 'the first centuries were his *beau ideal* of Christianity'. Not only did this formative influence not harmonise very well with Newman's Evangelicalism, but his 'imaginative devotion' to the Fathers 'saved him from the danger' of any serious attraction to latitudinarism after he had abandoned Evangelicalism, although he confessed to 'a certain disdain for Antiquity', including 'some flippant language against the Fathers' during those early years at Oriel under Whately's intellectual influence.[14]

In the summer of 1828 Newman began to read the Fathers systematically, beginning with the early Apostolic Fathers, for 'as I moved out of the shadow of that liberalism which had hung over my course, my early devotion towards the Fathers returned'.[15] Next year he wrote in a letter that he was 'so hungry for Irenaeus

[11] *Apo.* 26.
[12] *AW* 70–1.
[13] *Apo.* 20.
[14] *AW* 83; *Apo.* 25.
[15] *Apo.* 35.

and Cyprian' that ' I long for the Vacation'.[16] The row with the Provost of Oriel over the office of a college tutor, which came to a head in 1830 with Newman's enforced resignation, was a severe blow to Newman's strongly felt views on education (and therefore of significance eventually to his classic work *The Idea of a University*); however, not only was it a great relief from the point of view of his scholarly research, but it was of momentous importance for religious history because Newman's freedom from teaching duties meant leisure to study the Fathers, a profound and prolonged study that was crucial both for the Tractarian Movement and also for Newman's eventual conversion to the Roman Catholic Church. 'Humanly speaking', Newman later thought, the Oxford Movement 'never would have been, had he not been deprived of his Tutorship'.[17]

Tractarianism, which began formally in 1833 as a protest against Erastianism or state interference in the Church's affairs, soon developed into a much larger inquiry into the divine nature of the Catholic Church proclaimed in the historic creeds retained in the Church of England's liturgy after the Reformation. As such, it inevitably turned its attention to the great Fathers of the undivided Church of East and West. Newman's own first book, *The Arians of the Fourth Century* (1833), reflects his particular interest in the Eastern (especially the Alexandrian) Fathers. And indeed this was to be the predominant theological influence on him: to understand Newman's thought we must look to Athanasius not to Augustine, let alone Aquinas. The Protestant boy, the Evangelical adolescent, the liberal young don received his real formation in theology and spirituality not from the West but from the East. In a very real and important sense we can say that theologically Newman always remained closer to the Eastern Orthodox than to Latin Roman Catholics. It is not without interest that the first foreign soil he set foot on was Corfu on his Mediterranean tour of 1832–3, and so it was an Eastern Orthodox rather than Roman Catholic country that he first

---

[16] *LD* ii. 150.
[17] *AW* 96.

experienced. He was naturally extremely interested to observe a church which traced its origins to his own religious mentors, the Greek Fathers. Not surprisingly he found 'little objectionable . . . and much that was very good' in the liturgy.[18] He was particularly struck by the strong devotion to the Virgin Mary, which is more prominent in the Orthodox liturgy than in the Latin Mass.

However, it was to a country which owed its Christianity to Rome and which until the 16th century had been in communion with the Pope that Newman returned. And during the succeeding years it was inevitably the claim of the Roman Catholic Church to be identical with the One, Holy, Catholic, and Apostolic Church which the Church of England professed through the Creeds to believe in and of which the Tractarians insisted she was one of the three branches alongside Rome and Constantinople, that more and more engrossed Newman's attention. The sustained attempt to find a 'media via', or middle way for Canterbury between Geneva and Rome, forced him to undertake a detailed study of Tridentine theology with its heavily institutional ecclesiology. In the event, his submission to Rome in 1845 was not primarily an acceptance of papal claims (although of course it involved them) but rather an acknowledgement that of all the Christian bodies only the Roman Catholic Church could claim to be the authentic and legitimate succession of the undivided Church of the Fathers. Newman was not converted to Catholicism because of some ideal of a church or out of disillusion with the Anglican Church. His conversion was first and foremost a recognition of the identity of the Roman Catholic Church – a church, apart from a few Eastern or so-called Uniate rites in communion, that was overwhelmingly Latin or Western – with the primitive, undivided Church.

When he became a Catholic, Newman had no intention of writing any more theology. Partly this was because at that time Catholic theology meant exclusively scholastic theology, that is the theology that derived ultimately from the medieval Schoolmen, although during the intervening centuries and since

[18] *LD* iii. 181.

the Council of Trent and the controversies of the Reformation the link with St. Thomas Aquinas, the 'Angelic Doctor', had become blurred and obscure. In the event, Newman found himself unable to keep clear of ecclesiological problems as he tried to make his contribution on the apologetic and educational fronts. His own conception of the Church naturally included the essential hierarchical and institutional elements of the Tridentine Church but it also included other elements drawn from Eastern theology and his Anglican experience. Reluctantly, Newman was drawn into controversy as the Ultramontane movement to secure the definition of papal infallibility gathered force. The resulting theology of the Church was, apart from his theory of doctrinal development, his major contribution to Catholic theology, which was more than vindicated by the centrepiece of the Second Vatican Council, *Lumen Gentium,* the great constitution on the Church.

In the four chapters that follow I shall consider the negative as well as the positive elements in the Christian traditions that Newman experienced before his conversion to Catholicism. These different formative influences he came to consider to be more or less approximations to or distortions of the fullness of Christianity which he found in the Catholic Church. As I have pointed out, Newman's religious development encompasses in a remarkable way all the main varieties of the Christian religion to be found in the world today, although clearly his exposure to Eastern Christianity came from books rather than from personal contact.

In Chapter 6 I shall show how Newman's two main objections to Roman Catholicism in the end turned into decisive arguments for the claims of the Church of Rome. The final chapter, 7, examines the ways in which Newman's call for reform in the Catholic Church has been fulfilled by the Second Vatican Council, and how the positive elements in the non-Catholic varieties of Christianity, as Newman experienced them, have still to contribute to the more perfect and effective realisation of the fullness of Christianity in Catholicism.

2

Bible Christianity

To the majority of people living in a predominantly Protestant country, it would seem self-evident that Christianity is a religion that takes its origin and its form from the Bible. The story of a Catholic priest visiting an English house and being politely informed, 'No, there are no Roman Catholics here, we're all Christians' makes the point pithily enough. In a society and culture where it is taken for granted that the only yardstick for discovering and determining the nature of the Christian religion must be the Bible, it is very odd indeed to suggest that there may be other criteria. Whatever the Reformation failed to achieve, it has certainly had the effect of indelibly impressing the popular mind with the notion of 'the Bible and only the Bible'.

Until comparatively recently, large numbers of people in English-speaking countries at least regularly attended churches of several denominations who would have thought of themselves as Protestants first and foremost, only secondarily as Anglicans or Methodists. This would certainly have been the case with the Newman family. Christian worship consisted primarily of the reading of the Scriptures, the singing of psalms and hymns, and preaching. The service of Holy Communion was very rarely celebrated. Creeds and sacraments were not prominent. Such undogmatic Protestantism, without any of the enthusiasm of Evangelicalism, has been steadily on the wane throughout the century to the point of imminent extinction.

It would be wrong to imply that this type of Protestantism is necessarily anti-dogmatic. Rather, it is undogmatic because the question of dogma is largely unexamined and secondary to what is perceived as the ethical message of the Gospel. To be a Christian is to act in accordance with the central moral precepts

9

of the New Testament rather than to believe anything in particular. Christian discipleship is seen as primarily following what is taken to be the moral example of Jesus, while doctrine is seen as irrelevant or distracting. To say, however, that dogma is totally absent from this kind of Christianity would be to exaggerate. Newman himself, as we have seen, acknowledged that his Evangelical conversion meant 'a returning to, a renewing of, principles' which he had '*already* felt, and in a measure acted on' – although it was not till he was 15 that he 'fell under the influences of a definite Creed, and received into my intellect impressions of dogma'.[1]

There is an obvious sense in which a dogma-less Christianity may be very attractive. In *The Arians of the Fourth Century* Newman even says that, far from dogmatic formulations of Christian belief being desirable for their own sake, in fact 'freedom from symbols and articles is abstractedly the highest state of Christian communion, and the peculiar privilege of the primitive Church', for 'technicality and formalism are, in their degree, inevitable results of public confessions of faith', whereas 'when confessions do not exist, the mysteries of divine truth, instead of being exposed to the gaze of the profane and uninstructed, are kept hidden in the bosom of the Church, far more faithfully than is otherwise possible'. However, Newman recognises that dogmatic definitions are both inevitable and necessary, even if 'the rulers of the [early] Church was dilatory in applying a remedy, which nevertheless the circumstances of the time imperatively required. They were loath to confess, that the Church had grown too old to enjoy the free, unsuspicious teaching with which her childhood was blest.'[2]

Newman's lack of enthusiasm here for dogma was partly the result of the important theological principle that human language is of its very nature inadequate to express God's revelation. This was involved in his discovery of the early Church's principle of so-called *economy*. His study of the Alexandrian Church introduced him to the theology of Clement and Origen, which was 'based on the mystical or sacramental

[1] *Apo.* 17.
[2] *Ari.* 36–7.

principle, and spoke of the various Economies or Dispensations of the Eternal'. Accordingly, the Church's 'mysteries are but the expressions in human language of truths to which the human mind is unequal'.[3]

The principle of economy[4] meant that the doctrine of the Trinity, for example, is to be seen only as 'the shadow, projected for the contemplation of the intellect, of the Object of scripturally-informed piety: a representation, economical; necessarily imperfect, as being exhibited in a foreign medium and therefore involving apparent inconsistencies or mysteries'. 'Systematic' dogma could be 'kept in the background in the infancy of Christianity, when faith and obedience were vigorous', and only 'brought forward at a time when, reason being disproportionately developed, and aiming at sovereignty in the province of religion, its presence became necessary to expel an usurping idol from the house of God'. From the point of view of the individual believer, to make explicit what was implicit was not necessarily desirable: 'So reluctant is a well-constituted mind to reflect on its own motive principles, that the correct intellectual image, from its hardness of outline, may startle and offend those who have all along been acting upon it.' But having indicated how undesirable dogmatic formulations are, Newman immediately proceeds to show how necessary they are: for the fact that 'we cannot restrain the rovings of the intellect, or silence its clamorous demand for a formal statement concerning the Object of our worship', means paradoxically that the insistence that 'intellectual representation should ever be subordinate to the cultivation of the religious affections' actually demands the 'intellectual expression of theological truth,' not only because it 'excludes heresy', but because it 'directly assists the acts of religious worship and obedience'.[5]

In *Tract 73* (1835), later republished under the title 'On the Introduction of Rationalistic Principles into Revealed Religion', Newman explains why human language is inherently incapable

[3] *Apo.* 36–7.
[4] For the following discussion of revelation, see Ian Ker, *Newman on Being a Christian* (Notre Dame: University of Notre Dame Press, 1990; London: Harper Collins, 1992), 23–9.
[5] *Ari.* 145–6.

of expressing adequately the truths of divine revelation. 'Considered as a Mystery', a revealed truth 'is a doctrine enunciated by inspiration, in human language, as the only possible medium of it, and suitably, according to the capacity of language; a doctrine *lying hid* in language, to be received in that language from the first by every mind, whatever be its separate power of understanding it.' He takes the necessity of verbal formulations for granted, but he also recognises the inevitable inadequacy of language and the limitations of human thought. He formulates a brilliant exposition of how mystery is involved in the idea of revelation:

> No revelation can be complete and systematic, from the weakness of the human intellect; so *far as* it is not such, it is mysterious . . . A Revelation is religious doctrine viewed on its illuminated side; a Mystery is the selfsame doctrine viewed on the side unilluminated. Thus Religious Truth is neither light nor darkness, but both together; it is like the dim view of a country seen in the twilight, with forms half extracted from the darkness, with broken lines, and isolated masses. Revelation . . . is not a revealed *system*, but consists of a number of detached and incomplete truths belonging to a vast system unrevealed, of doctrines and injunctions mysteriously connected together.[6]

In *Lectures on the Doctrine of Justification* (1838), doctrinal statements are still seen as negative rather than positive. Necessary and useful as 'landmarks' and summaries of belief, they are 'intended to forbid speculations, which are sure to spring up in the human mind, and to anticipate its attempts at systematic views by showing the ultimate abyss at which all rightly conducted inquiries arrive, not to tell us anything definite and real, which we did not know before, or which is beyond the faith of the most unlearned'.[7]

By the time, however, Newman came to write the last of the *Oxford University Sermons* on 'The Theory of Developments in Religious Doctrine' (1843), the formulation of dogmatic propositions is viewed in a more positive light, if only because doctrinal development is seen as a sign of life in the Church. It is

[6] *Ess.* i. 41–2.
[7] *Jfc.* 316.

true that doctrinal statements are said to be 'necessary only because the human mind cannot reflect . . . except piecemeal' upon 'the one idea which they are designed to express', so that they are only expressions of 'aspects' of the 'idea' and 'can never really be confused with the idea itself, which all such propositions taken together can but reach, and cannot exceed', and indeed to which they 'are never equivalent' – for 'dogmas are, after all, but symbols of a Divine fact, which, far from being compassed by those very propositions, would not be exhausted, nor fathomed, by a thousand'. On the other hand, dogmatic definitions are regarded as essential for realising the Christian revelation. There is no contradiction between a personal faith in Christ and a dogmatic creed, because the latter only seeks to give expression and substance to the former:

> That idea is not enlarged, if propositions are added, nor impaired if they are withdrawn: if they are added, this is with a view of conveying that one integral view, not of amplifying it. That view does not depend on such propositions: it does not consist in them; they are but specimens and indications of it. And they may be multiplied without limit. They are necessary, but not needful to it, being but portions or aspects of that previous impression which has at length come under the cognizance of Reason and the terminology of science . . . One thing alone has to be impressed on us by Scripture, the Catholic idea, and in it they are all included. To object, then, to the number of propositions, upon which an anathema is placed, is altogether to mistake their use; for their multiplication is not intended to enforce many things, but to express one.[8]

If this view of revelation (the 'idea') seems too impersonal, then it is important to look at the later passage in the *Grammar of Assent* where Newman provides a classic statement of the relation between a personal faith and doctrinal belief, criticising 'the common mistake of supposing that there is a contrariety and antagonism between a dogmatic creed and vital religion':

> People urge that salvation consists, not in believing the propositions that there is a God, that there is a Saviour, that our Lord is God, that there is a Trinity, but in believing in God, in a Saviour, in a Sanctifier; and they object that such propositions

[8] *US* 331–2, 336

are but a formal and human medium destroying all true reception of the Gospel, and making religion a matter of words or of logic, instead of its having its seat in the heart. They are right so far as this, that men can and sometimes do rest in the propositions themselves as expressing intellectual notions; they are wrong, when they maintain that men need do so or always do so. The propositions may and must be used, and can easily be used, as the expression of facts, not notions, and they are necessary to the mind in the same way that language is ever necessary for denoting facts, both for ourselves as individuals, and for our intercourse with others. Again, they are useful in their dogmatic aspect as ascertaining and making clear for us the truths on which the religious imagination has to rest. Knowledge must ever precede the exercise of the affections. We feel gratitude and love, we feel indignation and dislike, when we have the information actually put before us which are to kindle those several emotions. We love our parents, as our parents, when we know them to be our parents; we must know concerning God, before we can feel love, fear, hope, or trust towards Him. Devotion must have its objects; those objects, as being supernatural, when not represented to our senses by material symbols, must be set before the mind in propositions. The formula, which embodies a dogma for the theologian, readily suggests an object for the worshipper.[9]

We have come a long way from *The Arians,* where dogma was seen as hardly more than a necessary evil, to a position where doctrinal formulations are viewed as indispensable for personal faith. It is not just that dogma protects religion from error, but doctrinal propositions are now viewed as integral to faith itself, which can hardly exist without some knowledge of what it seeks to worship. Of course, Newman knew when he wrote *The Arians* that the believer cannot worship Christ without knowing something of his divinity; but he seemed to have thought that it was a pity Christianity could not rest in the simplest kind of proclamation of faith, without any dogmatic developments at all. Thirty-seven years later, he is anxious both to explain and to refute this attitude. Newman's final position is that far from there necessarily being an opposition between a personal and a propositional religion, the two should be mutually interdependent.

[9] *GA* 82–3.

But because dogmatic propositions are implied by an objective religion does not mean that it is possible, or even desirable, to list all the doctrines which a Catholic at any given time has to believe. The Church, Newman points out, 'would be misrepresenting the real character of the dispensation' and 'abdicating her function' by transferring the faith of Catholics 'from resting on herself as the organ of revelation . . . simply to a code of certain definite articles or a written creed'.[10] The Catholic position is that 'the object of faith is *not* simply certain articles . . . contained in the dumb documents, but the whole word of God, explicit and implicit, as dispensed by His living Church'.[11] A Catholic cannot itemise the contents of revelation, since

> there are many things which we know on the whole, but of which we cannot tell the boundaries. I know what is morally right, yet I cannot draw a sharp line in matters of detail between what is right and what is wrong. And so there may be points in Revelation which do not positively and undeniably command my faith, while yet there are points which certainly do.

Newman uses a striking secular analogy to describe the Church as the expounder and interpreter of revelation: it is like 'a standing Apostolic committee – to answer questions, which the Apostles are not here to answer, concerning what they received and preached'. But because 'the Church does not know more than the Apostles knew, there are many questions which the Church cannot answer'.[12] The Church, however, has to be infallible since Christianity 'is no mere philosophy thrown upon the world at large, no mere quality of mind and thought, no mere beautiful and deep sentiment or subjective opinion, but a substantive message from above, guarded and preserved in a visible polity'. It was because God 'willed the Gospel to be a revelation acknowledged and authenticated, to be public, fixed, and permanent', that 'He framed a Society of men to be its home, its instrument, and its guarantee', so that the 'rulers of that Association are the legal trustees, so to say, of

[10] *LD* xxiii. 99–100.
[11] *LD* xxiii. 105.
[12] *LD* xxv. 418.

the sacred truths which He spoke to the Apostles by word of mouth'.[13]

Newman's study of primitive Christianity had shown him that the early Church did not use the Scriptures to teach the revelation of Christ, but rather that the Church itself taught what was to be believed, and only appealed to 'Scripture in vindication of its own teaching': heretics, on the other hand, like the Arians, relied on a 'private study of Holy Scripture' to elicit 'a systematic doctrine from the scattered notices of the truth which Scripture contains'.[14] The more Newman as an Anglican studied the Fathers, the more he became aware that the Bible was used by them to support the doctrines which they received from the Church's tradition, which was itself regarded as the interpreter of the Scriptures.

The idea that 'every one may gain the true doctrines of the gospel for himself from the Bible', he called the 'ultra-Protestant principle'; whereas according to the Fathers, 'the unanimous witness of the whole Church' to the teaching of the apostles was 'as much the voice of God' as was Scripture.[15] To insist, Newman argues, on 'the Bible as the only standard of appeal in doctrinal inquiries' inevitably leads to the conclusion that 'truth is but matter of opinion', since 'the Bible is not so written as to force its meaning upon the reader', nor does it 'carry with it its own interpretation'. To be sure, Newman thought as an Anglican that the 'creed can be proved entirely . . . from the Bible' – but 'we take this ground only in controversy, not in teaching'. And he readily admits that Christians 'derive their faith' not from Scripture but from tradition.[16] Anyway there are serious problems in trying to draw doctrines directly and solely from the Bible, which, although inspired, is like other books in its 'history' and in the 'mode of its composition', and which in fact is 'not one book' but 'a great number of writings, of various persons, living at different times, put together into one, and assuming its existing form as if casually and by accident'. To attempt to deduce 'the true system of religion' from such an unsystematic 'collection' would be

[13] *Diff.* ii. 236, 322.
[14] *Ari.* 50–1.
[15] *LD* v. 166.
[16] *VM* i. 26–7, 245, 28, 244.

like trying 'to make out the history of Rome from the extant letters of some of its great politicians, and from the fragments of ancient annals, histories, law, inscriptions, and medals'. The writers of the New Testament 'did not sit down with a design to commit to paper all they had to say' about the gospel; they wrote with more limited, specific purposes in mind. Indeed, they themselves acknowledge that they 'did not in Scripture say out all they had to say', but they actually refer to a 'system' of doctrine and worship which would have survived even if Scripture had been lost. Not surprisingly, then, the 'doctrines of faith' are in Scripture 'only in an implicit shape'.[17]

If a Biblical Christianity is wrong to underplay dogma and if dogmas anyway are taught not by the Scriptures but by the Church, is there anything positive to be learned from this kind of Christianity? As a Catholic, Newman came to think very decidedly that there was a considerable advantage compared with a religion where the Church in practice tended to supersede Scripture. For if, unlike the Church, the Bible was never intended to teach doctrines as such – after all, 'a book does not speak; it is shut till it is opened'[18] – still, it is immensely important for a faith that comes from the heart as well as the head. Many years of experience as a Catholic taught Newman that his first impressions of the simple, objective faith of Catholics was only one side of the picture. The fact was that Catholics themselves were dependent on the Gospels for their picture of Christ and that Catholicism must practically – not to say doctrinally – be a Biblical Christianity. The Bible, he wrote,

> is the best book of meditations which can be, because it is divine. This is why we see such multitudes in France and Italy giving up religion altogether. They have not impressed upon their hearts the life of our Lord and Saviour as given us in the Evangelists. They believe merely with the intellect, not with the heart. Argument may overset a mere assent of the reason, but not a faith founded in a personal love for the Object of Faith. They quarrel with their priests, and then they give up the Church. We can quarrel with men, we cannot quarrel with a book.[19]

[17] *DA* 146–8, 150–1.
[18] *SN* 53.
[19] *LD* xxvi. 87.

There are, after all, advantages in 'a book', provided we do not try to make it do something which by its nature it cannot do. Since Vatican II Catholics have been enthusiastically encouraged to read the Bible. The former distinct discouragement was, of course, based on the fear that the Scriptures might be used in place of the Church as the Protestant Reformers had advocated. The danger of neglecting the voice of the living Church and of tradition in favour of 'a book' which obviously cannot interpret itself still exists. But the profit for Catholics of having their imaginations steeped in the events of the life of Christ is enormous. As Newman put it succinctly in a note for a sermon, 'to know Christ is to know Scripture'.[20] And this is indeed the very first religious formation that the young Newman as a boy received. The problem arises when we try to deepen and enhance our knowledge of this Person, for that inevitably demands a further knowledge in the form of doctrines which do not, so to speak, spring out of the pages of Scripture, although ultimately they can be traced back to it. Nor is the person of the incarnate, crucified, and risen Christ only to be found in the pages of the gospels: he is also to be found in the eucharistic liturgy and sacraments of the Church which Protestantism tends to ignore or at least undervalue.

[20] *SN* 230.

3

Evangelical Christianity

Before considering Newman's sustained critique of Evangelicalism, it is important to stress the positive elements of this part of his religious development.

First of all, it was the conversion of 1816 which 'made me a Christian', he later wrote.[1] What was involved above all was a commitment to a doctrinal religion: 'I fell under the influences of a definite Creed, and received into my intellect impressions of dogma, which, through God's mercy, have never been effaced or obscured.'[2] His own experience was not at all exceptional, for Evangelical 'teaching had been a great blessing for England', since 'it had brought home to the hearts of thousands the cardinal and vital truths of Revelation'.[3]

Second, there was the significance of conversion. Looking back at the end of his life, Newman found it 'difficult to realise or imagine the identity of the boy before and after August 1816' – he seemed to be 'another person'.[4] The personal experience of conversion to Christ is, of course, the hallmark of Evangelical Christianity which, whatever its shortcomings, has never neglected evangelisation, whether of unbelievers or of nominal Christians. Newman, indeed, saw conversion as the instrument of other conversions: 'The sight of a convert is the most cogent and withal the most silent and subduing of arguments.'[5] His own life revolved around his two great conversions of 1816 and 1845, so that his own Christianity was deeply marked by the

[1] *AW* 268.
[2] *Apo.* 17.
[3] *AW* 79.
[4] *LD* xxxi. 31.
[5] *LD* xi. 224.

experience of conversion, which is inevitably more and more a feature of Christians in a post-Christian society.

The third element worth emphasising is that of a personal, living faith. Newman came to reject theologically the classic Evangelical distinction between so-called 'nominal' and 'real' Christians: he ceased to believe that it was possible to distinguish the really converted Christians from the unregenerate. His experience of working as a curate in an Oxford parish had shown him that Evangelicalism was 'unreal' and 'not a key to the phenomena of human nature'.[6] Nevertheless a preoccupation with a *real* Christian faith runs through his Anglican sermons. Thus, for example, he preached that most Christians do not 'realise' what it is they profess to believe, but remain in 'an unreal faith', substituting 'a mere outward and nominal profession' for 'real' belief. For it is the 'indolent use of words without apprehending them' which is the natural concomitant of a merely 'passive faith'. If religion 'must be *real*', then to profess Christianity as true, and yet not be able to 'feel, think, speak, act as if it were true', is to believe 'in an unreal way'. The reason, then, why people do not 'act upon the truths they utter' is 'because they do not *realise* what they are so ready to proclaim'. It is only when people 'realise a truth' that 'it becomes an influential principle within them'.[7] In this kind of insistent preoccupation with a *real* Christianity one can see very clearly the formative influence of Evangelicalism. And yet Newman ends by turning this very Evangelical theme against itself as he proceeds to explore more deeply the nature of religious unreality, as we can see in the following analysis which may serve to introduce his severe criticism of Evangelical theory and practice.

In one of the most penetrating sermons he ever preached, 'Unreal Words' (1839), Newman pointed out that when we subscribe to religious beliefs, we have to use words and 'Words have a meaning, whether we mean that meaning or not', so that 'To make professions is to play with edged tools, unless we attend to what we are saying.' The expression of religious feelings, too, may be unreal, since someone may '*not* really

---

[6] *AW* 79.
[7] *PS* i. 17, 54, 81; ii. 29, 179; v. 31; vi. 95, 263.

believe' the doctrines of Christianity 'absolutely, because such absolute belief is the work of long time, and therefore his profession of feeling outruns the real inward existence of feeling, or he becomes unreal'. Newman even concludes that 'unreality . . . is a sin; it is the sin of every one of us, in proportion as our hearts are cold, or our tongues excessive'.[8] It was not coldness of heart but an excess of feeling and words which Evangelicals were likely to be guilty of. If justification by faith was the one cardinal doctrine of the gospel there was likely to be a tendency to exaggerate one's emotional response to the offer of personal salvation, just as the depreciation of works was calculated to exaggerate the importance of words.

In *The Arians of the Fourth Century,* Newman argues that Evangelicals who appeal to Christ's death on the cross to arouse the kind of emotion that is likely to lead to conversion do the very opposite to the early Fathers whose 'uniform method' was 'to connect the Gospel with Natural Religion, and to mark out obedience to the moral law as the ordinary means of attaining to a Christian faith'. The reticence of the primitive Church – the principle of economy or reserve – in concealing the Christian mysteries stood in marked contrast to the way in which Evangelicals 'publicly . . . canvass the most solemn truths in a careless or fiercely argumentative way; truths, which it is as useless as it is unseemly to discuss in public, as being attainable only by the sober and watchful, by slow degrees, with dependence on the Giver of wisdom, and with strict obedience to the light which has already been granted'. Again, the early Church, far from relying on a 'private study of Holy Scripture' to elicit 'a systematic doctrine from the scattered notices of the truth which Scripture contains', only appealed to 'Scripture in vindication of its own teaching'.[9]

When the first volume of *Parochial Sermons* was published in 1834, Newman was criticised by Evangelicals for allegedly neglecting the role of the Holy Spirit in the Christian life. Although (as we shall see) Newman had in fact a very high doctrine of the Holy Spirit, there was some truth in the charge.

---

[8] *PS* v. 33, 39, 43.
[9] *Ari.* 46–7, 136–7, 50–1.

For he was deliberately reacting against an Evangelical spirituality which stressed regeneration at the expense of sanctification. The reason why he preached in the way that he did was because he believed the Holy Spirit normally works through ordinary human channels, such as conscience, reason, and feelings, and 'does not come immediately to change us' – 'the awful and eternal truth' being 'that our hearts must be changed for heaven and can but be slowly changed'. It was in this sense that he could go so far as to say that 'salvation depends on ourselves'. And so in his preaching he had been 'led' to 'enlarge on our part of the work not on the Spirit's'. It was quite true that Christian works had to be done 'through the Spirit'; but that did not alter the fact that they had to be done by ordinary human means. Evangelicalism led people to assume 'that a saving state is one, where the mind merely looks to Christ', with the result that actual moral behaviour could seem virtually irrelevant.[10]

There was another aspect of Evangelical spirituality that Newman strongly criticised in his preaching, and that was its tendency to introversion: 'Instead of looking off to Jesus, and thinking little of ourselves, it is at present thought necessary . . . to examine the heart with a view of ascertaining whether it is in a spiritual state or not.' The 'inherent mischief' of the Evangelical theory of justification by faith lies 'in its necessarily involving a continual self-contemplation and reference to self'. Newman explains:

> He who aims at attaining sound doctrine or right practice, more or less looks out of himself; whereas, in labouring after a certain frame of mind, there is an habitual reflex action of the mind upon itself . . . for, as if it were not enough for a man to look up simply to Christ for salvation, it is declared to be necessary that he should be able to recognise this in himself . . .

It was a strange paradox that a theology which insisted on the absolute impossibility of any kind of self-justification should end in a complacent, not to say arrogant, self-sufficiency:

> He who has learned to give names to his thoughts and deeds, to appraise them as if for the market, to attach to each its due

[10] *LD* v. 14–16, 22.

measure of commendation or usefulness, will soon involuntarily corrupt his motives by pride or selfishness. A sort of self-approbation will insinuate itself into his mind: so subtle as not at once to be recognised by himself . . ."

Newman was well aware that his own sermons were criticised for their coldness, but then he did not set the same store by preaching as the Evangelicals did. It was not so much verbal homilies as concrete sacraments which were intended to influence and persuade people, for the latter were 'the great persuasives of the Gospel, as being visible witnesses and substitutes for Him who is Persuasion itself'. He thought anyway that preaching was not the way to convert people but the way to prepare them for conversion. Evangelical preachers certainly could 'melt' the hearts of their hearers, but the effect was in the long term superficial – only 'a blaze among the stubble'. Exciting emotions was not the same as convincing people. Newman's depreciation of the power of sermons comes oddly from one of the greatest of Christian preachers. Before the publication of the second volume of his *Parochial Sermons* in 1835, he expressed doubt about the value of sermons in general, feeling that 'real profit' is 'the exception not the rule'. Inevitably, they had to be formal and impersonal rhetorical addresses. But Evangelical sermons were positively harmful in 'their rudeness, irreverence, and almost profaneness . . . of making a most sacred doctrine' like the atonement 'a subject of vehement declamation, or instrument of exciting the feelings, or topic for vague, general, reiterated statements in technical language'. He thought it was 'inexpressibly' distressing to hear 'our Lord's name and work used as a sort of charm or spell to convert men by, not in the selfabasement of prayer and praise, but in the midst of rhetorical flourishes or at best in an unreal mechanical way'. Very different had been 'the rule of the Primitive Church, of teaching the more Sacred Truths ordinarily by rites and ceremonies', which 'persuade' by their 'tenderness and mysteriousness', while they are 'prepared for' by a 'severity of preaching' that should 'enlighten the mind as to its real state' and ' dig round about the Truth'. It was far more 'reverential' that the doctrines of

---

" *PS* ii. 171.

Christianity should be inculcated through sacraments rather than sermons. Above all, the eucharist was 'the continual revelation of the Incarnation' and it was the neglect of this central sacrament in conventional Protestantism that had caused, he felt, the enthusiasm of the Evangelical revival, 'which had the ardour and some of the depth of the Old Catholic Doctors, without their reverence, sanctity, and majesty'.[12]

Psychologically speaking, Newman felt that revivalist preaching in the end tended to undermine faith. The recipients of this kind of reiterated appeal to the feelings became emotionally 'worn out'. For 'if we say things over without feeling them, we become worse not better. Children, who are taught, since they were weaned, to rely on the Christian atonement, and in whose ears have been dinned the motives of gratitude to it etc before their hearts are trained to understand them, are deadened to them by the time they are 21.' Emphasising 'Christian motives' all the time, in a way the Apostles never did, claims Newman, 'leads ultimately to no men feeling them'.[13]

We may think that in the heat of Tractarian agitation for the restoration of the primacy of the sacraments in Anglicanism Newman underestimated the power of preaching. Certainly there can be no question that his own preaching from the pulpit of the University Church of St. Mary the Virgin made a decisive contribution to the Oxford Movement. Anyway, as we have seen, Newman did not deny the importance of preaching in preparing people for receiving Christ in the sacraments. Had he been writing as a Catholic, he might have written even more favourably in the light of the undeniable fact that Catholics, thanks to deficient catechesis and evangelisation, are often significantly 'over-sacramentalised'. Evangelicals suffered from a different kind of over-exposure to emotional pressures. But this was not the only factor that could easily lead to an abandonment of orthodox Christianity.

One particular problem with the preoccupation with the atonement and justification by faith was not only that it undervalued the importance of moral works but that it tended

[12] *LD* v. 32, 45–7.
[13] *LD* ii. 308.

to put other aspects of the Christian faith in the shade. The resulting indifference to doctrines not directly connected with the one great Evangelical concern was a neglect of dogma in general. It was not therefore surprising that Newman could write, 'the Children of evangelical parents . . . will generally turn liberals'.[14] Indeed, he thought that Evangelicalism led directly to rationalism in religion, the moral basis of which was that the 'Rationalist makes himself his own centre, not his Maker'. This 'narrow and egotistic temper of mind', he feared, was 'the spirit' that was pervasive: 'Instead of looking out of ourselves, and trying to catch glimpses of God's workings, from any quarter, – throwing ourselves forward upon Him and waiting on Him, we sit at home bringing everything to ourselves, enthroning ourselves in our own views, and refusing to believe anything that does not force itself upon us as true.' The result was that 'the idea of Mystery' was 'discarded', and religion became subjective rather than objective. Writing in 1835, Newman is happy to lay the blame squarely on Evangelicalism, which directs 'its attention to the heart itself, not to anything external to us, whether creeds, actions, or ritual', so that it 'is really a specious form of trusting man rather than God', and consequently 'in its nature Rationalistic'. The liberal theology of Schleiermacher, he added, was the inevitable 'result of an attempt of the intellect to delineate, philosophise, and justify that religion (so called) of the heart and feelings, which has long prevailed.'[15]

What Newman called the 'principle of private judgement' in interpreting Scripture was certainly not exclusive to Evangelicals, but as the dominant and dogmatic wing of Protestantism they bore a special responsibility for the effect on doctrinal orthodoxy. He warned (correctly, as it turned out) his brother Francis that his Evangelicalism would lead him into unbelief, since the 'ultra-Protestant principle' that 'every one may gain the true doctrines of the gospel for himself from the Bible' meant that he would ultimately 'unravel the webb of selfsufficient inquiry'[16] Evangelicals claimed Scripture as the authority for

---

[14] *LD* ii. 308.
[15] *Ess.* i. 33–4, 36, 95–6.
[16] *LD* v. 166.

their understanding of Christianity, but who was to say that their interpretation of the Bible was truer than that of Roman Catholics, for example, who rested their interpretation on the authority of the Church?

The legitimate exercise of private judgment, the Anglican Newman argued, lay in ascertaining 'not what has God revealed, but whom has He commissioned?' The Scriptures 'sanction, not an inquiry about Gospel doctrine, but about the Gospel teacher'. When, therefore, 'an appeal *is* made to private judgment, this is done in order to settle who the teacher is and what are his notes or tokens, rather than to substantiate this or that religious opinion or practice'. Since St. Paul tells us that the Church is our teacher, the 'simple question . . . for Private Judgment to exercise itself upon is, what and where is the Church?' All this was not surprising:

> Religion is for practice, and that immediate. Now it is much easier to form a correct and rapid judgment of persons than of books or of doctrines. Every one, even a child, has an impression about new faces; few persons have any real view about new propositions . . . The multitude have neither the time, the patience, nor the clearness and exactness of thought, for processes of investigation and deduction. Reason is slow and abstract, cold and speculative; but man is a being of feeling and action . . .[17]

Christ had founded a Church which was one, holy, Catholic, and Apostolic. The question was: where, if anywhere, was it to be found? Recognition of this Church need not involve complex scriptural and theological arguments, as its notes should be discernible. In his novel *Loss and Gain* (1848), Newman humorously explains that converts to the Catholic Church have, of course, to use their 'private judgment' in order to find the true Church – but

> they use it in order ultimately to supersede it; as a man out of doors uses a lamp in a dark night, and puts it out when he gets home. What would be thought of his bringing it into his drawing room? . . . if he came in with a great-coat on his back, a hat on his head, an umbrella under his arm, and a large stable-lantern in his hand?[18]

[17] *Ess.* ii. 350–1, 353.
[18] *LG* 203.

Evangelicalism, however, not only calls upon people to recognise the Scriptures as the Word of God but also upholds in theory the right of the individual to interpret the Bible. But this right is not in practice allowed to permit any divergence from the doctrine of justification by faith, in particular. As Newman puts it sarcastically, the sixteenth-century Reformers had used their 'private judgment' against the Catholic Church, but 'There was enough of private judgment in the world, they thought, when they had done with it themselves. So they forcibly shut-to the door which they had opened, and imposed on the populations they had reformed an artificial tradition of their own, instead of the liberty of inquiry and disputation.'[19]

Newman's most trenchant criticism of Evangelical theology is to be found in his *Lectures on the Doctrine of Justification* (1838), specifically the last chapter called 'On Preaching the Gospel'. There Newman maintains that Protestantism – 'having fallen, after the usual manner of self-appointed champions and reformers, into the evil which it professed to remedy' – is itself guilty of the very charge of *'legalism'* which it wrongly makes against 'Catholic Truth'. It charges that just as 'Judaism interposed the Mosaic Law between the soul and Christ . . . so the Christian Church, Ancient and Catholic, also obscures the right and true worship of Him . . . by insisting on Creeds, on Rites, and on Works'.[20] By rejecting 'what has been actually given', Protestantism was 'sure to adopt what had not been given'. Thus Protestants 'congratulate themselves on their emancipation from forms and their enlightened worship, when they are but in the straight course to a worse captivity, and are exchanging dependence on the creature for dependence on self'. Ironically, 'they substitute faith for Christ', and 'so regard it, that instead of being the way to Him, it is in the way'. Pithily, he insists: 'they make it a something to rest in . . . they alter the meaning of the word, as the Jews altered the meaning of the word Law . . . they have brought into the Gospel, the narrow, minute, technical, nay, I will say carnal and hollow system of the Pharisees.' With contemporary Evangelicals in mind, he elaborates:

[19] *Prepos.* 55.
[20] *Jfc.* 313–14.

a system of doctrine has risen up during the last three
centuries, in which faith or spiritual-mindedness is contemplated
and rested on as the end of religion instead of Christ . . . And in
this way religion is made to consist in contemplating ourselves
instead of Christ; not simply in looking to Christ, but in
ascertaining that we look to Christ, not in His Divinity and
Atonement, but in our conversion and our faith in those truths.

Such was the result of the obsession with justification by faith
alone. Instead of preaching Christ, the 'fashion of the day' is 'to
preach conversion', to tell people 'to be sure they look at Christ,
instead of simply holding up Christ to them', and 'to tell them
to have faith, rather than to supply its Object' – with the result
that 'faith and spiritual-mindedness are dwelt on as *ends,* and
obstruct the view of Christ'. It would be as if one were to 'affect
people by *telling* them to weep or laugh'. Rather than feeling
'spontaneously, as the consequence of the objects presented to
them', people 'will feel this and that, because they are told to feel
it'. This explains 'the absence of . . . composure, unobtrusiveness,
healthy and unstudied feeling, variety and ease of language,
among those who are thus converted, even when that conversion
is sincere.' Anyone who has met 'born again' Christians will
recognise the unmistakable symptoms that Newman describes in
his account of their self-preoccupation:

> Poor miserable captives, to whom such doctrine is preached as
> the Gospel! What! is *this* the liberty wherewith Christ has made
> us free, and wherein we stand, the home of our own thoughts,
> the prison of our own sensations, the province of self . . . This is
> nothing but a specious idolatry . . .[21]

As for the Reformers' strictures on 'conscience-stricken
Catholics' concerned to win salvation through their good works,
Newman remarks tersely and sarcastically, 'surely it is better not
to have Christ and to mourn, than to let Him go and to think it
gain'.[22] Evangelical Protestants picture faith 'as a sort of passive
quality which sits amid the ruins of human nature, and keeps up
what may be called a silent protest, or indulges a pensive
meditation over its misery' – whereas in fact:

[21] *Jfc.* 330.
[22] *Jfc.* 332–3.

> True faith is what may be called colourless, like air or water; it
> is but the medium through which the soul sees Christ; and the
> soul as little really rests upon it and contemplates it, as the eye
> can see the air. When, then, men are bent on holding it (as it
> were) in their hands, curiously inspecting, analysing . . . they are
> obliged to colour and thicken it, so that it may be seen and
> touched. That is, they substitute for it something or other . . .
> which they may hang over, and doat upon. They rather aim at
> experiences . . . within them, than at Him that is without them.

If our salvation consists in our being justified by faith, it is not
surprising if this faith becomes the object of our attention. Such
'being the difference', Newman concludes, 'between true faith
and self-contemplation, no wonder that where the thought of
self obscures the thought of God, prayer and praise languish,
and only preaching flourishes'.[23] Yet another sharp aphorism
sums up the argument: 'To look at Christ is to be justified by
faith; to think of being justified by faith is to look from Christ
and to fall from grace.' The reader is left with the great paradox:

> [Luther] found Christians in bondage to their works and
> observances; he released them by his doctrine of faith; and he left
> them in bondage to their feelings . . . for outward signs of grace
> he substituted inward; for reverence towards the Church
> contemplation of self. And . . . whereas he preached against
> reliance on self, he introduced it in a more subtle shape; whereas
> he professed to make the written word all in all, he sacrificed it in
> its length and breadth to the doctrine which he had wrested from
> a few texts.[24]

How far this kind of Protestantism is really attributable to
Luther is seriously questioned by modern scholars, but
Newman's critique remains a powerful indictment of popular
Evangelicalism.[25]

---

[23] *Jfc.* 336–7.

[24] *Jfc.* 339–40.

[25] A. E. McGrath, *Iustitia Dei: A Christian History of the Doctrine of
Justification* (Cambridge: Cambridge University Press, 1986), vol. ii, 121–34;
H. Chadwick 'The Lectures on Justification', in I. Ker and A. G. Hill, eds.,
Newman After a Hundred Years (Oxford: Clarendon Press, 1990), 287–308; H.
Chadwick, 'Newman's Significance for the Anglican Church' in D. Brown, ed.,
Newman: A Man for our Time (London: SPCK, 1990), 54–5.

The final moral is that this is 'what comes of fighting God's battles in our own way'; for just as the Pharisees, who 'were more careful of their Law than God who gave it', and Judas, who 'was concerned at the waste of the ointment, which might have been given to the poor', were 'bad men' who 'professed to be more zealous ... than the servants of God', so 'in a parallel way Protestants would be more spiritual'.[26] It was an arresting irony with which to complete his final, most sustained repudiation of what he scathingly called earlier

> this modern, this private, this arbitrary, this unscriptural system, which promising liberty conspires against it; which abolishes Christian Sacraments to introduce barren and dead ordinances; and for the real participation of the Son, and justification through the Spirit, would at the very marriage feast, feed us on shells and husks, who hunger and thirst after righteousness! It is a new gospel, unless three hundred years stand for eighteen hundred; and if men are bent on seducing us from the ancient faith, let them provide a more specious error, a more alluring sophism, a more angelic tempter, than this. It is surely too bold an attempt to take from our hearts the power, the fulness, the mysterious presence of Christ's most holy death and resurrection, and to soothe us for our loss with the name of having it.[27]

This chapter has been overwhelmingly negative, but our opening remarks on the positive elements in Newman's experience of Evangelical Christianity will come into their own later when we consider the Catholic Church's situation in the contemporary post-Christian society.

[26] *Jfc.* 340–1.
[27] *Jfc.* 57.

4

Liberal Christianity

On 12 May 1879 Newman gave his famous *biglietto* speech in Rome in response to his election to the College of Cardinals by Pope Leo XIII. He began the speech by referring to the 'many trials' he had suffered, trials (as everyone knew) which he had suffered at the hands of his Ultramontane opponents. He also remarked that the papal honour was intended not only to 'give pleasure to English Catholics' but 'even to Protestant England'. But this unashamed avowal of his own liberal Catholicism introduces an uncompromising attack on an altogether different kind of religious liberalism. This was the liberalism which he had described in the *Apologia* as 'false liberty of thought, or the exercise of thought upon matters, in which, from the constitution of the human mind, thought cannot be brought to any successful issue, and therefore is out of place', and which include first principles, especially religious ones that cannot be subjected to 'human judgment' because they are 'revealed doctrines which are in their nature beyond and independent of it'.[1] The implication of the speaker now is that the two kinds of liberalism are not to be confused, and that in his unswerving opposition to the latter kind Newman is completely at one with the Catholic Church.

> In a long course of years I have made many mistakes. I have nothing of that high perfection, which belongs to the writings of Saints, *viz.*, that error cannot be found in them; but what I trust that I may claim all through what I have written, is this, – an honest intention, an absence of private ends, a temper of obedience, a willingness to be corrected, a dread of error, a desire

[1] *Apo.* 256.

31

to serve Holy Church, and, through Divine Mercy, a fair
measure of success. And I rejoice to say, to one great mischief I
have from the first opposed myself. For thirty, forty, fifty years I
have resisted to the best of my power the spirit of liberalism in
religion. Never did Holy Church need champions against it more
sorely than now, when, alas! it is an error overspreading, as a
snare, the whole earth . . .

Once again Newman offers a definition of this kind of
liberalism:

Liberalism in religion is the doctrine that there is no positive
truth in religion, but that one creed is as good as another, and
this is the teaching which is gaining substance and force daily. It
is inconsistent with any recognition of any religion, as *true*. It
teaches that all are to be tolerated, for all are matters of opinion.
Revealed religion is not a truth, but a sentiment and a taste; not
an objective fact, not miraculous; and it is the right of each
individual to make it say just what strikes his fancy. Devotion is
not necessarily founded on faith. Men may go to Protestant
Churches and to Catholic, may get good from both and belong
to neither. They may fraternise together in spiritual thoughts and
feelings, without having any views at all of doctrine in common,
or seeing the need of them.

The resulting secularisation means that religion is no longer
considered 'the bond of society' since 'that goodly framework of
society which is the creation of Christianity, is throwing off
Christianity'.

Instead of the Church's authority and teaching, they would
substitute first of all a universal and a thoroughly secular
education, calculated to bring home to every individual that to
be orderly, industrious and sober is his personal interest . . . As to
Religion, it is a private luxury, which a man may have if he will;
but which of course he must pay for, and which he must not
obtrude upon others, or indulge in to their annoyance.

But since there is another kind of liberalism of which
Newman is very much in favour, he promptly makes the
important modification, 'that there is much in the liberalistic
theory which is good and true; for example, not to say more, the
precepts of justice, truthfulness, sobriety, self-command,
benevolence, which . . . are among its avowed principles, and the

natural laws of society'. On the other hand, again, it is precisely because of the positive aspects of this sort of liberalism that 'There never was such a device of the Enemy, so cleverly framed, and with such promise of success'.[2]

In this chapter I shall not, of course, be considering either Newman's advocacy of liberal education or his eventual espousal of relatively liberal political views, although these are obviously related to the theological liberalism which he was concerned as a Catholic to promote. It is this liberalism that I propose to set against the anti-dogmatic liberalism which he consistently opposed throughout his life both as an Anglican and as a Catholic. The question of whether or not Newman was a liberal Catholic is a recurring topic of debate. I hope to show as clearly and concisely as possible Newman's real position which is distinct from both the typical Catholic extremes of progressivism and integralism. That there was even in Newman's day a liberalism within the Catholic Church which was antipathetic to Newman in exactly the same way as liberal Protestantism is plain enough. But before looking at that, we must trace Newman's constant resistance to dogmatic liberalism within the Church of England.

The Anti-dogmatic Principle

At the beginning of the Oxford Movement, Newman became convinced that the Church of England must find a popular basis like the early Church, which had not depended on establishment but on the people. But in 1829, before the Tractarian agitation began, in the face of political reforms like Catholic emancipation which were threatening the Church's position, he realised that the modern democratic, secular society was conducive to an anti-dogmatic liberalism:

> We live in a novel era – one in which there is an advance towards universal education. Men have hitherto depended on others, and especially on the Clergy, for religious truth; now each man attempts to judge for himself. Now, without meaning of course that Christianity is in itself opposed to free inquiry, still I think it *in fact* at the present time opposed to the particular form

[2] *Campaign* 393–9.

which that liberty of thought has now assumed. Christianity is of faith, modesty, lowliness, subordination; but the spirit at work against it is one of latitudinarianism, indifferentism, republicanism, and schism, a spirit which tends to overthrow doctrine, as if the fruit of bigotry, and discipline as if the instrument of priestcraft.[3]

Newman was clear that since the 'tendency of the age is towards *liberalism*' and since religion has to be 'enforced by authority of some kind', it was the Church which was 'the *legitimate* enforcement of Christian truth. The liberals know this – and are in every possible manner trying to break it up.'[4] As his political thinking matured and developed, he came to see that mere negative reaction was counter-productive; and even earlier, as he deepened his knowledge of the Fathers, he came to feel, as I have said, that the Church must somehow again become a popular power. When he joined a Church that was free of state control and sure of its own authority, he stressed the crucial importance of the laity for the credibility of the Catholic Church. If dogmatic religion was to be effectively taught and practised, then the people of God themselves had a vital role to play. At any rate it was all too clear to the young Newman in his twenties that the spread of education and democracy inevitably involved a tendency towards religious liberalism, as the hierarchical Church lost much of its social power. Thus, in March 1831, he saw the writing on the wall as the new Whig administration began passing the Reform Bill through parliament. 'The vital question', he later wrote, was how 'to keep the Church from being liberalised'?[5]

In his study of the Arian heresy, Newman has contemporary religious liberals very much in mind. Arianism, unlike earlier heresies, was originally 'a sceptical rather than a dogmatic teaching', aiming 'to inquire into and reform the received creed, rather than to hazard one of its own', and as such enjoying all the advantages of 'the assailant' over 'the party assailed' in 'finding' rather than 'solving objections'.[6] In questioning the

[3] *LD* ii. 129–30.
[4] *LD* ii. 264–5.
[5] *Apo.* 39.
[6] *Ari.* 26–7.

orthodox creed, the Arians, too, were guilty of misapplying human reason to the mysteries of revelation. Furthermore, their objection to using 'words not found in Scripture, in confessions of faith' was of the very essence of the 'principle of liberalism'.[7] As for doctrinal 'comprehensiveness', Newman declares bluntly: 'If the Church would be vigorous and influential, it must be decided and plain-spoken in its doctrine ... To attempt comprehensions of opinion ... is to mistake arrangements of words, which have no existence except on paper, for ... realities; and ingenious generalisations of discordant sentiments for that practical agreement which alone can lead to co-operation.' While it is only realistic to accept that 'there are no two opinions so contrary to each other, but some form of words may be found vague enough to comprehend them both', comprehensiveness is impractical because it is unreal: 'We may indeed artificially classify light and darkness under one term or formula; but nature has her own fixed courses ... However plausible may be the veil thus thrown over heterogeneous doctrines, the flimsy artifice is discomposed as soon as the principles beneath it are called upon to move and act.' But comprehensiveness is, in fact, harmful to the Church, because of its unreal substitution of 'words for things', in the form of 'statements so faintly precise and so decently ambiguous, as to embrace the greatest number of opinions possible, and to deprive religion, in consequence, of its austere and commanding aspect'.[8] So much for those modern exercises in ecumenism which seek to paper over the cracks and to find lowest common denominators.

But the danger was real enough in Newman's own day. While on his Mediterranean cruise of 1832–3, he heard of the 'very comprehensive' plan of Dr. Thomas Arnold to reform the Church of England in order to prevent its disestablishment:

> If I understand it right, all sects (the Church inclusive) are to hold their meetings in the Parish Church – though not at the same hour of course. He excludes Quakers and Roman Catholics – yet even with this exclusion surely there will be too many sects in some places for one day? . . . If I might propose an

[7] *Ari.* 361–2.
[8] *Ari.* 147–8, 274.

amendment, I should say, pass an Act to oblige some persuasions to *change* the Sunday – if you have two Sundays in a week, it is plain you could easily accommodate any probable number of sects . . . Nor would you interfere with the Jews' worship (which of course is to be in the Church) – they are too few to take up a whole day. Luckily the Mohammedan holiday is already on a Friday; so there will be no difficulty of arrangement in that quarter.[9]

The witty sarcasm anticipates Ronald Knox's famous satire on 'Reunion All Round' (1914), as does a subsequent letter on the comparative illiberality of Dr. Arnold's scheme:

he is said to exclude the Jews, Roman Catholics, and Quakers from the Churches – this seems to me illiberal. The only objection I can fancy is the want of time in one day for these in addition to those already admitted to participation in the Churches – I am aware the Quakers remain an indefinite period at one sitting – and it would not do to keep the Sandemonians or the Socinians waiting – there must be a punctuality, if all are to be accommodated. Yet I think the difficulty might be met by forcing the Evangelicals to keep their Sunday on the Saturday . . . The Jews could take Saturday too – and the Roman Catholics would come in for Sunday in place of the Evangelicals. The Mahometan Feast being Friday would not interfere. – Or on the whole, since it is immaterial on what day the Christian festival is kept, the whole week might be divided among the various denominations of Christians. – I have another plan, which I hold to be altogether original and is the firstfruits of my late conversion and runs Dr A hard. It is to allot the 24 Colleges and Halls of Oxford among the various denominations – in this way you might meet the difficulty about subscription . . . I would allow of exchanges or conversions . . .[10]

With the *Tracts for the Times,* which began to appear in September 1833, the Oxford Movement may be said to have really and truly begun. They were Newman's idea and he threw himself into the work of writing, printing, and even personally distributing them. It is significant that he was quite ready to contact Evangelical as well as high church clergy, for his object was to rally opposition to 'the principles of Liberalism'[11]. Indeed,

[9] *LD* iii. 257–8.
[10] *LD* iii. 298.
[11] *Apo.* 49.

he blamed the rise of Evangelicalism on the 'lowminded' Latitudinarians or liberal Anglicans of the 18th century who had 'robbed the Church of all her more beautiful characteristics'.[12]

In *Tract 85*, he argues that unless Christianity 'contains no definite message, creed, revelation, system ... nothing which can be made the subject of belief at all', it is hard to take liberal Protestantism seriously: 'Why should God speak, unless He meant to say something? Why should He say it, unless He meant us to hear?' If there has been a revelation, then 'there must be some essential doctrine proposed by it to our faith'; and so it is difficult 'to be a consistent Latitudinarian', because even he will hold on to 'his own favourite doctrine, whatever it is'. It is surely against 'the common sense of mankind' to have 'a religion without doctrines': for 'Religion cannot but be dogmatic: it ever has been.'[13]

There was nothing at this time that irritated Newman more than that peculiarly Anglican brand of liberalism, a 'comprehensiveness' which is not so much an explicit denial of objective dogma as the attempt to hold together all dogmas, however irreconcilable, in a kind of flabby fusion:

> In the present day mistiness is the mother of wisdom. A man who can set down half a dozen general propositions, which escape from destroying one another only by being diluted into truisms, who can hold the balance between opposites so skilfully as to do without fulcrum or beam, who never enunciates a truth without guarding himself from being supposed to exclude the contradictory, who holds that Scripture is the only authority, yet that the Church is to be deferred to, that faith only justifies, yet that it does not justify without words, that grace does not depend on sacraments, yet is not given without them, that bishops are a divine ordinance, yet those who have them not are in the same religious condition as those who have, – this is your safe man and the hope of the Church; this is what the Church is said to want, not party men, but sensible, temperate, sober, well-judging persons, to guide it through the channel of No-meaning, between the Scylla and Charybdis of Aye and No.

---

[12] *LD* v. 21.
[13] *DA* 130–1, 134.

The history of Anglicanism indicates that Newman was wrong to suppose that this kind of all-embracing comprehensiveness has no future. People, he wrote,

> will not keep standing in that very attitude, which you please to call sound Church-of-Englandism or orthodox Protestantism. It tires them, it is so very awkward; and for the life of them they cannot continue in it long together, where there is neither article nor canon to lean against; they cannot go on for ever standing on one leg, or sitting without a chair, or walking with their legs tied, or grazing, like Tityrus's stags, on the air.[14]

But, as he knew very well, it was the alleged genius of Anglicanism 'to call it moderation and judgment to sit down deliberately between two stools, or to leap into the ditch, and ultraism to clear it'.[15] High Anglicans might, but ordinary English people did not ask the agonising question, 'Whom are we to believe? . . . How can that be practically a church, how can it *teach*, which speaks half a dozen things in the same breath?'[16]

Still, whatever the nature of Anglicanism, Newman felt that religious liberalism led to scepticism which in turn raised the possibility once again of a dogmatic faith. As he wrote to his brother Francis on 22 October 1840:

> Latitudinarianism is an unnatural state; the mind cannot long rest in it; and especially if the fact of a revelation be granted, it is most extravagant and revolting to our reason to suppose that after all its message is not ascertainable and that the divine interposition reveals nothing. The more scepticism abounds, the more is a way made for the revival of a strong ecclesiastical authority; Christianity arose in the beginning, when the popular religions had lost their hold upon the mind. So strongly do I feel this, that, averse as the English people are to Romanism, I conceive that did their choice lie in the mere alternative they would embrace even Romanism rather than acquiesce in absolute uncertainty. [17]

The continual stream of conversions to Roman Catholicism, particularly among intellectuals, in post-Protestant countries

---

[14] *Ess.* i. 302.
[15] *Ess.* i. 336
[16] Quoted in *Ker* 251.
[17] *Ker* 200.

throughout the 20th century, confirms Newman's prophecy. In the same countries, or at least in the English-speaking ones, the massive decline of traditional Protestantism has similarly opened up the way for the spread of fundamentalist Evangelicalism. Where there is a doctrinal void, as Newman saw, there will be an opportunity for the re-establishment of a more dogmatic religion. But that said, Newman knew well that so strong culturally has been the influence of a gentle, undoctrinal Anglicanism that 'It is not at all easy (humanly speaking) to wind up an Englishman to a dogmatic level.'[18]

In his *Essay on the Development of Christian Doctrine* (1845), which preceded his reception into the Roman Catholic Church, Newman maintained that 'a revelation is not given, if there be no authority to decide what it is that is given'. Consequently, there is a necessity for an infallible authority as opposed to the 'comprehension of opinions' which is the hall-mark of the Church of England.[19] Dogmatism, which is 'a religion's profession of its own reality as contrasted with other systems', must be a distinguishing principle of Christianity, which Newman describes as follows:

> That there is a truth then; that there is one truth; that religious error is in itself of an immoral nature; that its maintainers, unless involuntarily such, are guilty in maintaining it; that it is to be dreaded; that the reach for truth is not the gratification of curiosity; that its attainment has nothing of the excitement of a discovery; that the mind is below truth, not above it, and is bound, not to descent upon it, but to venerate it; that truth and falsehood are set before us for the trial of our hearts . . . this is the dogmatical principle . . .

Very different is the principle of liberalism –

> That truth and falsehood in religion are but matter of opinion; that one doctrine is as good as another; that the Governor of the world does not intend that we should gain the truth; that there is no truth; that we are not more acceptable to God by believing this than by believing that; that no one is answerable for his opinions; that they are a matter of necessity or accident; that it is

[18] *Apo.* 185.
[19] *Dev.* 89–90.

enough if we sincerely hold what we profess; that our merit lies in seeking, not in possessing; that it is a duty to follow what seems to us true, without a fear lest it should not be true; that it may be a gain to succeed, and can be no harm to fail; that we may take up and lay down opinions at pleasure; that belief belongs to the mere intellect, not to the heart also; that we may safely trust to ourselves in matters of Faith, and need no other guide . . .[20]

Several key points emerge from this uncompromising comparison: first, that there is such a thing as objective truth in religion; second, that the moral element is integral to the search for religious truth, both in the sense that we are to be held morally responsible for what we believe, and in the sense that our religious views are of the utmost moral importance; third, that although religious truth is not something that we just decide for ourselves without any authoritative guide, nevertheless it is attainable personally by the individual; fourth, that sincerity is not enough; fifth, that a vague pilgrimage towards an indefinite destination is not the same as the serious search for truth; sixth, that religious faith involves the whole person not just a part of the person. Any contemporary religious discussion such as can be viewed weekly on television, for instance, will show how far the spirit of liberalism in Newman's senses is taken for granted by the participants and those involved in the media. And it is, of course, the Catholic and the fundamentalist who are portrayed as eccentric in their insistence on the need for authority and on the immutability and objectivity of truth.

In England, where the Church of England is still the established religion, this liberalism is likely to take the form of that Anglican kind of comprehensiveness which characterises the Christian body that contains within it the most disparate theological views ranging from crypto-papalism to Evangelical fundamentalism. In the first book he published (anonymously) as a Catholic, a novel *Loss and Gain* (1848), Newman marvellously satirises the boundless comprehensiveness of Mr. Vincent, a college tutor who eulogises the Church of England as follows:

---

[20] *Dev.* 357–8.

'Our Church,' he said, admitted of great liberty of thought within her pale. Even our greatest divines differed from each other in many respects; nay, Bishop Taylor differed from himself. It was a great principle in the English Church. Her true children agree to differ. In truth, there is that robust, masculine, noble independence in the English mind, which refuses to be tied down to artificial shapes, but is like, I will say, some great and beautiful production of nature – a tree, which is rich in foliage and fantastic in limb, no sickly denizen of the hothouse, or helpless dependent of the garden wall, but in careless magnificence sheds its fruits upon the free earth, for the bird of the air and the beast of the field, and all sorts of cattle, to eat thereof and rejoice.'[21]

In Newman's view true Anglicanism, that is the religion of the essentially political and non-theological English Reformation, or rather Elizabethan settlement, is historically a kind of compromise between Catholicism on the one hand and Protestantism on the other. As such, it appeals, as it were, to 'the good sense of mankind', refusing 'to run into extremes' on the ground that the 'human mind is naturally prone to excess'. It is this comprehensive, essentially liberal Christianity that is the real religion of the Church of England – 'It is this, or it is nothing; deny this, and it forthwith dissolves into Catholicism or Protestantism.'[22]

Newman, however, did not consider this Anglicanism actually to be the popular religion of the country: 'the [historical] Church of England's religion is not the religion of England.' Rather, the religion of the people was that very Bible religion in which he himself had been brought up. This was what he though was so serious about *Essays and Reviews,* the famous collection of essays by liberal Anglicans published in 1860. In fact, his own response to the book was much more nuanced and subtle than the typical, predictable orthodox and progressive reactions. As we shall see, his own approach to this *cause célebre* reflected his own complex attitude as a Catholic to the delicate question of church authority. He was certainly not opposed to theological speculation, provided it was published in academic

[21] *LG* 84–5.
[22] *Diff.* ii. 374.

journals and not broadcast abroad in a way calculated to disturb ordinary people's faith. This kind of religious controversy would not have been such a problem in an earlier age, but in the modern world 'every one is alive to religious subjects' – the 'growth of scepticism' was 'appalling' and 'Christianity is tending to go out in whole classes'. Moreover, anything, Newman saw very clearly, that threatened the popular view of the Bible was calculated to have the most serious effect on religious belief.

> The religion of England is 'the Bible, the whole Bible, and nothing but the Bible' – the consequence is that to strike a blow at its inspiration, veracity or canonicity, is directly to aim at whatever there is of Christianity in the country. It is frightful to think where England would be, as regards Revelation, if it once got to disbelieve or to doubt the authority of Scripture.

This was but 'one illustration' of why he could not 'defend Christianity on the Anglican basis'. It was true that a Catholic has to believe in the inspiration of Scripture, but then 'the Church has defined very little upon the subject ... and we should have a sufficient ground of faith and teacher of doctrine, though ... the whole Bible were miraculously to vanish out of the world'. Not only does a Catholic believe 'in the word of God thro' His Church', but, he added significantly, 'there is nothing which binds the Catholic to belief in various portions of Genesis etc as popularly interpreted'.

He wondered if the contributors to *Essays and Reviews* saw 'the termination, or rather the abyss, to which these speculations lead', and whether they realised that, 'before attempting to sift facts, they ought to make sure that they have a firm hold of true and eternal principles. To unsettle the minds of a generation, when you give them no landmarks and no causeway across the morass is to undertake a great responsibility.' To people who took it for granted that Christianity was a religion one found in the Bible, the meaning and truth of the Scriptures was a matter of 'life and death'.[23] Nowadays, of course, scepticism and unbelief are far more prevalent than in Newman's day and the literal truth of the Bible, especially the Old Testament, is not assumed in the way it would have been in Newman's day.

---

[23] *LD* xix. 480, 482–3, 485, 487–8.

Nevertheless, the furore, to take the most notorious recent example, that has greeted the Bishop of Durham's denials of the virginal conception and physical resurrection, reveals all too clearly the force of Newman's words. Not only was the Bishop apparently casting doubt on the belief of many ordinary Christians, but in questioning the status of fundamental, apparently historical facts in the New Testament he was also necessarily raising the whole question of authority. To liberals like Bishop David Jenkins, of course, there is no ultimate authority, nor need there be, nor (doubtless) should there be: it is up to each individual Christian to arrive at their own beliefs by consulting the Bible in the light of modern knowledge and with the private guidance of the 'Spirit' – in practice, the spirit of the age rather than the Holy Spirit. Liberals, like Evangelicals, assume that the Bible is the ultimate basis of Christianity, but in their eyes it is not the same kind of authority but merely a point of reference. The momentous implications for many members of the Church of England, and indeed for the larger part of the British public who take it for granted that the Bible provides Christians with the content and evidence for their beliefs, have become only too apparent in the outcry that has followed the highly publicised views of the Bishop of Durham. The problem may be less acutely felt than in Newman's day, but that is because the Church of England has become progressively liberalised in the way he forecast it would.

The 'Religion of Civilisation'

Before turning to consider the nature of Newman's liberal Catholicism, it is not irrelevant to look at what he had to say about what he called the 'Religion of Civilisation'.[24] Newman thought that this kind of religion can be found as much among professed Christian believers as unbelievers. It is not in fact concerned explicitly with doctrine, but it may be regarded as a sort of psychological or spiritual counterpart to doctrinal liberalism. In the eighth discourse of *The Idea of a University*, where we find the celebrated portrait of the 'gentleman', Newman sees it as the potential result of the 'liberal' education

[24] *Idea* 158.

he is extolling. The word 'liberal' here has nothing to do with what we mean by religious liberalism but is used as the opposite of a vocational training. Nevertheless the tendency of such an education can create a cast of mind which is obviously closely allied to anti-dogmatic liberalism, as a result of ignoring rather than denying dogma. Since what are in question are attitude and behaviour rather than specific beliefs, the kind of doctrines that are likely to be neglected are:

> the ruined state of man; his utter inability to gain Heaven by any thing he can do himself; the moral certainty of his losing his soul if left to himself; the simple absence of all rights and claims on the part of the creature in the presence of the Creator; the illimitable claims of the Creator on the service of the creature; the imperative and obligatory force of the voice of conscience; and the inconceivable evil of sensuality. I speak of it as teaching, that no one gains Heaven except by the free grace of God, or without a regeneration of nature; that no one can please Him without faith; that the heart is the seat both of sin and of obedience . . .[25]

Newman uses other expression like the 'Religion of Reason' and the 'Religion of Philosophy' which indicate the intellectual origin of this frame of mind. If we substitute the word humanism, we have a contemporary phenomenon which approximates closely enough to what Newman is describing. For it is only too clear how insidiously a certain secular humanism can seep into the assumptions and preconceptions of Christians. It is not, as Newman says, that any particular dogma is denied; it is just that dogma is ignored or downgraded. For example, social justice is a laudable objective for Christians to pursue, but implicit (or not so implicit) identification of individual sin with social sin constitutes a fundamental rejection of Christian dogma. Or again there is a kind of self-destructive guilt which calls for a Christian affirmation of the dignity and worth of the individual; but there is a noticeable tendency in much contemporary spirituality for this kind of self-affirmation to slide into an implicit denial of the need for repentance and contrition. It is this sort of liberal humanism which undermines

[25] *Idea* 159.

the whole Christian doctrine of original sin and redemption. It is, of course, omnipresent now in liberal Protestantism, but one can see it very easily too in a post-Vatican II Catholicism which has overreacted against an excessively individualistic Catholicism with a special preoccupation with sexual weaknesses at the expense of sins against charity. Newman was protesting against the polite culture or cult of the gentlemanly that characterised his elitist society. Today we have to be on our guard against a perfectly commendable humanism which exalts the values of contemporary Western society above other values, as can be seen so easily in the patronising attitude of the first world to the third world, so poor in the goods and rights valued by the West but so rich in its family life and sense of community.

Newman thought that the hall-mark of the humanism he was warning against was its substitution of the moral sense for the conscience:

> Conscience indeed is implanted in the breast by nature, but it inflicts upon us fear as well as shame; when the mind is simply angry with itself and nothing more, surely the true import of the voice of nature and the depth of its intimations have been forgotten, and a false philosophy has misinterpreted emotions which ought to lead to God. Fear implies the transgression of a law, and a law implies a lawgiver and judge; but the tendency of intellectual culture is to swallow up the fear in the self-reproach, and self-reproach is directed and limited to our mere sense of what is fitting and becoming. Fear carries us out of ourselves, whereas shame may act upon us only within the round of our own thoughts. Such, I say, is the danger which awaits a civilized age; such is its besetting sin (not inevitable, God forbid! or we must abandon the use of God's own gifts), but still the ordinary sin of the Intellect; conscience tends to become what is called a moral sense; the command of duty is a sort of taste; sin is not an offence against God, but against human nature.

In an analogous way, we may say that the culture of our society places such a emphasis on social justice and human rights that there is the constant danger that these typically liberal virtues, which may indeed be of Christian inspiration and origin, become sulf-sufficient ends in themselves. In other words, caring and compassion cease to exemplify the supreme virtue of charity, that is love of God and neighbour, and become merely secular values.

Looking at certain contemporary Christians, we can certainly echo Newman's indictment, 'The less amiable specimens of this spurious religion are those which we meet not unfrequently in my own country.'[26] These Christians may not be obviously liberals in an anti-dogmatic sense, but the authentic spirit of Christian charity has been subtly pervaded by liberal humanistic values which are not necessarily by any means incompatible but which are essentially distinct. However, this is not surprising when one considers how indistinguishable in practice these very values often seem to be from Christian ones, the difference lying in the intention, motivation, and sense of priorities. Newman himself speaks in the most glowing terms of the

> influences, which intellectual culture exerts upon our moral nature, and all upon the type of Christianity, manifesting themselves in veracity, probity, equity, fairness, gentleness, benevolence, and amiableness; so much so, that a character more noble to look at, more beautiful, more winning, in the various relations of life and in personal duties, is hardly conceivable, than may, or might be, its result, when that culture is bestowed upon a soil naturally adapted to virtue. If you would obtain a picture for contemplation which may seem to fulfil the ideal, which the Apostle has delineated under the name of charity, in its sweetness and harmony, its generosity, its courtesy to others, and its depreciation of self, you could not have recourse to a better furnished *studio* than to that of Philosophy, with the specimens of it, which with greater or less exactness are scattered through society in a civilized age.[27]

Indeed, he is perfectly happy to admit that this liberal humanism may actually play a part 'in the conversion of man and the renovation of his nature', since 'even divine grace, to speak of things according to their appearances, is ordinarily baffled' – for

> Religion seems too high and unearthly to be able to exert a continued influence upon us: its effort to rouse the soul, and the soul's effort to co-operate, are too violent to last. It is like holding out the arm at full length, or supporting some great weight, which we manage to do for a time, but soon are exhausted and succumb.[28]

[26] *Idea* 165.
[27] *Idea* 164.
[28] *Idea* 160.

Just as Newman writes of the 'series of influences, which intellectual culture exerts upon our moral nature, and all upon the type of Christianity, manifesting themselves in veracity, probity, equity, fairness, gentleness, benevolence, and amiableness; so much so, that a character more noble to look at, more beautiful, more winning, in the various relations of life and in personal duties, is hardly conceivable'[29] – so too we could easily think of many contemporary humanists who, without any specifically Christian motivation, bravely and generously commit themselves to the struggle for human rights or for an amelioration of third world poverty. Sometimes, to quote Newman again, they 'seem able to fulfil certain precepts of Christianity more readily and exactly than Christians themselves'. The reason is that the 'world is content with setting right the surface of things; the Church aims at regenerating the very depths of the heart'.[30] Such moral characteristics of Newman's 'cultivated intellect' or of contemporary liberal humanism may indeed be found, as Newman says, 'within the pale of the Church', but even as they 'partly assist', so also they 'partly distort the development of the Catholic'.[31]

It seemed right to spend some time on this rather elusive point, not only because it is a recurring topic in Newman's writings, but because it is surely a very significant, if not at all obvious, aspect of the religious liberalism he is opposing. For him certainly Christianity is 'ever civilisation . . . but, unhappily, in matter of fact, civilization is not necessarily Christianity', if it remains merely 'a second-rate perfection of nature, being what it is, and remaining what it is, without any supernatural principle', instead of 'that perfection which nature aims at, and requires, and cannot of itself reach'.[32] This religion of civilisation may, of course, have a veneer of Christianity on it when this is socially acceptable or demanded, in which case its devotees 'accept it, they add it to what they *are*, they ingraft it upon the selfish and

[29] *Idea* 164.
[30] *Idea* 174.
[31] *Idea* 181.
[32] *HS* i. 165–6.

worldly habits of an unrenewed heart'.[33] But, as Newman explains in his well-known sermon 'The Religion of the Day', they take only one part of the gospel, that is, 'the brighter side of the Gospel, – its tidings of comfort, its precepts of love; all darker, deeper views of man's condition and prospects being comparatively forgotten'.

And here we touch on a slightly different aspect of Newman's attack on liberalism. Again, it is not exactly that any particular dogma is being impugned or questioned, but rather that one side of Christianity is being exaggerated at the expense of another. Every age, every culture, of course, is likely to emphasise different features of the Christian revelation. As Newman points out, there have been times when the 'darker side of the Gospel: its awful mysteriousness, its fearful glory, its sovereign inflexible justice' have practically excluded the love of God. But, *mutatis mutandis*, one can safely say that our own times are not very different from Newman's in a preoccupation with 'the brighter side of the Gospel'. All that has changed is that an elegant, polite, elitist society has been replaced by a more socially concerned, 'caring', egalitarian society, where compassion has replaced refinement as the supreme virtue. There is the same secularisation of conscience, except that it is now replaced by the social rather than moral sense, and the same liberalisation of ideas of divine justice. Is Newman's religion of civilisation all that different from the 'caring' tolerance of contemporary religious indifferentism?

> Every thing is bright and cheerful. Religion is pleasant and easy; benevolence is the chief virtue; intolerance, bigotry, excess of zeal, are the first of sins. Austerity is an absurdity; – even firmness is looked on with an unfriendly, suspicious eye.

Another characteristic of modern society is the proliferation of information and the growth of technology; inevitably in this climate

> religion will commonly seem to be dull, from want of novelty. Hence excitements are eagerly sought out and rewarded. New objects in religion, new systems and plans, new doctrines, new preachers, are necessary to satisfy that craving which the so-called

[33] *PS* i. 30.

spread of knowledge has created. The mind becomes morbidly sensitive and fastidious; dissatisfied with things as they are, desirous of change *as such* as if alteration must of itself be a relief.

This prevailing ethos encourages a liberalisation of religion as traditional doctrines and spirituality become suspect rather than recommended by their antiquity. Or again, the pursuit of material progress, of improving people's standard of living are perfectly laudable aims. But what to Newman is intolerable is to identify the 'vision of Christ's Kingdom with . . . mere human civilisation', particularly when the means used are based on 'unchristian principles'.

The reason why this kind of liberal humanism can be so insidious a threat to the gospel is precisely because 'it takes a general colouring from Christianity, so as really to be modified by it, nay, in a measure enlightened and exalted by it'. Indeed, Newman goes so far as to say that 'Satan has so composed and dressed out what is the mere natural produce of the human heart under certain circumstances, as to serve his purposes as the counterfeit of the Truth'. Still, he is ready to admit that 'many persons in whom this bad spirit shows itself, are but partially infected by it, and at bottom, good Christians, though imperfect'.

Summing up his antipathy to this watered-down kind of Christianity, Newman's sermon concludes with the defiant words 'I will not shrink from uttering my firm conviction, that it would be a gain to this country, were it vastly more superstitious, more bigoted, more gloomy, more fierce in its religion, than at present it shows itself to be.' It is not that these qualities are 'desirable . . . but I think them infinitely more desirable and more promising than . . . a cold, self-sufficient, self-wise tranquillity'. However, again there is the difficulty that there is a tranquillity which is certainly very much a note of the Christian, but which has very different causes. Appearances are deceptive when it comes to distinguishing the reality behind them, so that, Newman remarks, in 'the present religion of the educated world, full as it is of security and cheerfulness, and decorum, and benevolence, I observe that these appearances may arise either from a great deal of religion, or from the absence of it; they may be the fruits of shallowness of mind and a blinded conscience, or of that faith which has peace with God through our Lord Jesus Christ'.[34] As he remarks in one of his Catholic sermons, 'nature may counterfeit grace, nay even to the deception of the man himself in whom the counterfeit occurs'.[35] The test between the real thing and the sham must be an interior one, since it is the difference in motives and intention which is the crucial factor.[36]

Such is the subtle corruption of true Christianity, a theme to which Newman so often returns in his writings. He saw it as the typical fruit of a liberal education divorced from religious faith. We can identify an equivalent phenomenon in our own time, which is to be attributed generally to the rise of liberal humanism. Neither in Newman's day nor in ours is humanism to be rejected, but, as Newman would insist, a secular humanism, however similar it may look, is in fact quite distinct from a religious humanism, with which it is ultimately incompatible and to which it may in the last analysis be deeply inimical. But just as the potent attraction of the antiChrist, as Newman was wont to point out, must lie in his close resemblance to Christ, so too liberal humanism looks from the outside only too confusingly – and therefore dangerously – like Christian humanism. Such a religion of humanism is the natural religion of the liberal Christian who discounts dogma. It is not surprising that this kind of liberal will be heard making vehement declarations on the political and social issues of the day, but their voice is muted when it comes to other questions of morality. One cause of this is no doubt of a doctrinal nature, but the other factor is that the priorities and preoccupations of a secular humanism have succeeded in eclipsing or at least distorting the priorities of the Gospel.

Liberal Catholicism

It is time to conclude this chapter by examining in what ways and to what extent Newman may be called a liberal Catholic. In the broad sense, we could say that he began to entertain liberal views as early as 1846, almost exactly a year after his conversion,

[34] *PS* i. 311–13, 315–16, 320–1.
[35] *Mix.* 151.
[36] *OS* 23.

when he went to Rome to study for the Catholic priesthood at the College of Propaganda, which was then run by the Jesuits. Newman found them unthinkably conservative and deplored the narrow, unstimulating atmosphere of the seminary.[37] The next important discovery came when he went to Dublin as first President of the new Catholic University of Ireland and found that the bishops and clergy paid scant attention to the views of the laity. Laymen were to be 'treated like good little boys' and 'told to shut their eyes and open their mouths'.[38] So fraught with tension was the situation that he came to the conclusion that the 'fearful' breach between clergy and laity constituted the principal threat to the university's survival.[39] It was in fact Newman's sense of frustration at this clerical refusal to allow lay people their proper role in the life of the Church that led to his first theological writing as a Catholic.

At the beginning of 1857 Newman began to be dragged into the troubled affairs of the *Rambler*, the liberal Catholic periodical, when he wrote to the editor on the one hand to express disapproval of an article he thought theologically unorthodox, and on the other hand to commiserate with him over episcopal criticism of the *Rambler's* advocacy of raising Catholic educational standards. The incident was typical of Newman's attempt to occupy the middle ground between the so-called liberal Catholics and the Ultramontanes, that is extreme papal Catholics. In the end, he was forced to take on the editorship temporarily as the only compromise candidate acceptable to both the bishops and the management of the *Rambler*. While disapproving of the tone and the more extreme views put forward in the magazine, he nevertheless very much approved of its policy of openness, and not least its championing of the rights of the laity, for example in matters of education. It was in fact a passage written by himself as acting editor that initiated the controversy that was to make him an object of suspicion with the Roman authorities for so many years. In his view the bishops should

[37] See *Ker* 331.
[38] *AW* 328.
[39] *LD* xvii. 514.

really desire to know the opinion of the laity on subjects in which the laity are especially concerned. If even in the preparation of a dogmatic definition the faithful are consulted, as lately in the instance of the Immaculate Conception, it is at least as natural to anticipate such an act of kind feeling and sympathy in great practical questions . . .[40]

In his famous article 'On Consulting the Faithful in Matters of Doctrine' (1859), which he wrote especially for the *Rambler* in order to give a theological treatment of the laity, he defended his use of the word 'consult', which he says in ordinary English 'includes the idea of inquiring into a matter of *fact*, as well as making a judgment'. Thus, for example, 'a physician consults the pulse of his patient; but not in the same sense in which his patient consults *him*'. It is in the former sense that the Church 'consults' or 'regards' the faith of the laity before defining a doctrine. True, the laity's 'advice, their opinion, their judgment on the question of definition is not asked', nevertheless 'the matter of fact, viz. their belief, *is* sought for, as a testimony to that apostolical tradition, on which alone any doctrine whatsoever can be defined'.[41]

Although, as critics have pointed out, Newman was not using the word 'consult' in its more usual English sense, nevertheless he was certainly using the word in a perfectly acceptable sense, and it is hard to see what other word he could in fact have used. Still, it cannot be denied that his terminology has been the source of much confusion. Indeed, it is commonly supposed that Newman thought that the pope and bishops should 'consult', that is, take the advice of the laity before teaching or defining authoritatively. And because Newman *did* think that the hierarchy should, in this sense, certainly consult with lay people on non-doctrinal matters that are the laity's concern, the confusion has only increased. However, not only is the English word as much to blame as Newman, but of course in practice the two senses may be extremely close. When Pope Paul VI set up a commission to investigate the question of birth control, he included among its membership married couples who were to be

---

[40] *LD* xix. 129.
[41] *Cons.* 54–5.

'consulted' presumably as to their own experience in marriage rather than for their expertise in moral theology. And yet clearly rigid, hard-and-fast distinctions are rather hard to apply in practice, as the difference between fact and opinion is not always clear-cut. However, Newman was not thinking of doctrinal teaching in practical, moral matters but in defining points of revelation, where the only kind of 'opinion' that would be relevant would be on the timeliness or advisability of making a definition. To imagine that Newman thought that the teachings of the Church depended on Gallup polls would be a complete distortion of his actual liberalism as a Catholic.

Now this liberalism is not only to be found in the practical sphere, for there *was* a very important theological point that Newman was making, and that was really about the constitution or nature of the Church. Newman himself made the point in a humorous informal way when he recorded a conversation he had with his bishop, who 'said something like "Who are the laity?" I answered that the Church would look foolish without them . . . '[42] This was so not only for very obvious, practical reasons, but also for a profounder theological reason. For the laity, he wrote, must be consulted 'because the body of the faithful is one of the witnesses to the fact of the tradition of revealed doctrine, and because their *consensus* through Christendom is the voice of the Infallible Church'. There are 'channels of tradition', through which 'the tradition of the Apostles, committed to the whole Church . . . manifests itself variously at various times', none of which 'may be treated with disrespect', even though the hierarchy has sole responsibility for 'discerning, discriminating, defining, promulgating and enforcing any portion of that tradition'. He himself wanted 'to lay great stress on the *consensus fidelium*' in order to compensate for 'whatever deficiency there might be of patristical testimony on behalf of various points of the Catholic dogma'.[43]

Newman's first theological work as a Catholic, then, evinces very strikingly the way in which he was and was not a liberal Catholic. And the key to the distinction lies in his theological approach, which was both creative and traditional.

[42] *LD* xix. 141.
[43] *Cons.* 63–4.

Newman's negative experience in Dublin was not confined to the role of the laity. It was there that he felt the full impact of an authoritarian Church, in which bishops were 'so accustomed to be absolute that they usurp the rights of others, and rough ride over their wishes and their plans'.[44] Years later he wondered whether 'Bishops fancy that, as justice does not exist between the Creator and His creatures, between man and the brute creation, so there is none between themselves and their subjects'.[45] Still bishops themselves were 'moved . . . in automaton fashion from . . . Rome'.[46] The loss of the temporal power of the papacy, which so alarmed most of his co-religionists, left Newman unmoved: not even the prospect of a break in communications disturbed him, for 'it would cut off a great deal of unprofitable gossip sent to Rome . . . and of crude answers sent back from Rome by men who seem to have authority, but have none – and it would throw power into the hands of the local Bishops everywhere'.[47] The inevitable bureaucracy of a centralised authority had only increased with the steady rise of Ultramontanism during the nineteenth century. And it was not until the Second Vatican Council that many legitimate powers were restored to bishops. Ultramontanism, as it had developed from being an appeal 'across the Alps' to Rome for protection for the local church against state control to being a movement to place the papacy on an altogether different level from the episcopate, not only encouraged the growth of the Roman Curia's power but also was both the cause and the result of a reactionary retreat from the modern world in the wake of the French Revolution and in the face of modern democracy and secularisation. Newman thought that the loss of its temporal power would liberate the papacy from its dubious secular trappings, a view that seemed to imply that he was to be counted among liberal Catholics. But he also thought that a political revolution in Rome could only do good:

> . . . I view with equanimity the prospect of a thorough routing out of things at Rome – not till some great convulsions take place . . .

[44] *AW* 293.
[45] *LD* xxii. 293.
[46] *LD* xvii. 415 n. 2.
[47] *LD* xxii. 317.

and religion is felt to be in the midst of trials, red-tapism will go out of Rome, and a better spirit come in ... At present things are in appearance ... effete ... We are sinking into a sort of Novatianism, the heresy which the early Popes so strenuously resisted. Instead of aiming at being a world-wide power, we are shrinking into ourselves, narrowing the lines of communion, trembling at freedom of thought, and using the language of disarray and despair at the prospect before us, instead of, with the high spirit of the warrior, going out conquering and to conquer.[48]

If we wanted to personalise the issue, we could quote Newman's memorably gloomy words about the long pontificate of Pius IX, a pope whom he personally liked but who had failed to check the excesses of the Ultramontane extremists: 'We have come to a climax of tyranny. It is not good for a Pope to live 20 years. It is anomaly and bears no good fruit; he becomes a god, has no one to contradict him, does not know facts, and does cruel things without meaning it.'[49]

By the time Newman wrote these words, the doctrine of papal infallibility had been defined by the First Vatican Council. He had never opposed the dogma, properly understood and in the moderate form in which it had been defined, but he had considered its definition inopportune. Now he was prepared to accept its providential nature. In relation to the excesses of the Ultramontanes Newman was a liberal, but he was very much a conservative in the sense of being an old-fashioned Ultramontane like the French thinker Montalembert, who now seemed positively to be a liberal. Certainly Newman was convinced that the freedom of the local church from state control depended on the external authority of Rome. He reminded liberal Catholics, who were amazed at his readiness to concede power to the papacy, that the Oxford Movement had begun as a protest against Erastianism, the heresy which attributed power to the state over the Church. It was true that he had 'always inclined to the notion that a General Council was the magisterial exponent of the Creed', but, unfortunately, it had to be admitted that 'a General Council may be hampered and hindered by the action of infidel Governments upon a weak or

[48] *LD* xxii. 314–15
[49] *LD* xxv. 231.

time-serving episcopate'. This argument weighed so strongly with Newman that he was prepared to admit that

> It is . . . better that the individual command of Christ to Peter to teach the nations, and to guard the Christian structure of society, should be committed to his undoubted successor. By this means there will be no more of those misunderstandings out of which Jansenism and Gallicanism have arisen, and which in these latter days have begotten here in England the so-called Branch Theory . . .[50]

It was the same mandate naturally which had been given to the Apostles as a body that had also been conferred singly on Peter.

It was characteristic, however, of Newman's balance and ability to see all sides of the question that he was also only too aware of the danger of what is called 'creeping infallibility'. The immediate practical effect of the definition, carefully and moderately couched as it was, was little short of momentous: 'considered in its effects both upon the Pope's mind and that of his people, and in the power of which it puts him in practical possession, it is nothing else than shooting Niagara.' It would surely be hard to deny that Vatican I led to an undue concentration of power in the hands of the pope, which in practice meant the Roman Curia. But Newman was sure that a balance would re-assert itself: 'Remedies spring up naturally in the Church, as in nature, if we wait for them.'[51]

As a Catholic Newman was no more ready to side with liberal Catholics than with the Ultramontanes. He found the position of the German church historian, Ignaz von Döllinger, who refused to accept the infallibility definition, both indefensible and inexplicable. Not only did Döllinger (exactly like his Ultramontane enemies) grossly exaggerate what had actually been defined, but (the opposite was true of the Ultramontanes) he paid too much attention to and expected too much from history, which it was no more legitimate to appeal to against the Church than it was permissible to interpret Scripture by one's own private judgment against the authority of the Church. The

---

[50] *LD* xxv. 259.
[51] *LD* xxv. 278.

faith of a Catholic must be in the living voice of the Church not in Scripture or in historical investigation. Indeed, Newman points out, anyone 'who believes the dogmas of the Church only because he has reasoned them out of History, is scarcely a Catholic'.[52]

The open hostility of the dominant Ultramontane party to Newman was parallelled by the resentment that liberal Catholics like Lord Acton came to feel towards someone whose support they counted on in the struggle against the repression of Church authority. Because of the Second Vatican Council, even the most conservative Catholics can hardly denounce Newman as heretical, but he continues to be regarded with suspicion in some liberal quarters. Post-conciliar progressivists are much more likely to attack Newman for what they see as his servile attitude to authority. Those, on the other hand, who feel that the truth is more likely to lie in the mean between the extremes, see in Newman a prophetic figure, not just for the Council but for its troubled aftermath.

This kind of careful, nuanced balance is to be seen early on in the 1850s when Newman was trying to support the *Rambler*. Thus he applauded an article by Acton on the kind of individual liberty which the Catholic doctrine of conscience demanded, a freedom that was better observed in Protestant England than in some Catholic countries. This was a daring comparison to make when it is remembered that before the Second Vatican Council religious liberty was not even explicitly or officially recognised by the Catholic Church as either desirable or permissible in practice in countries where Catholicism was the official religion, on the ground that error (regardless of the people in error) had no rights. But Newman was less than pleased by the readiness of the *Rambler* to criticise the authorities of the Church. Highly critical himself of the misuse of authority, he was nonetheless even prepared to allow that there was some excuse for Roman authoritarianism: the 'position of the Holy See must be considered, especially in a missionary country', where it 'has to act, to act promptly and forcibly, and is forced to use such instruments as come to hand', to 'adopt courses which are

[52] *Diff.* ii. 312.

immediately effective, and measure services by what is showy, telling, and successful'.[53] It was highly characteristic of Newman to see all sides of the question and it shows how facile it is to try and neatly categorise him as either conservative or liberal.

But whatever his own difficulties and whatever his complaints about its abuse, Newman was always adamant not only on the abstract principle but also on the practical rights of authority. For what was the point of subscribing to the theory of the episcopate if one disallowed its exercise? He insisted, just as he would have done as an Anglican, that 'What a Bishop says is law to those over whom he has jurisdiction.' Still, a careful distinction had to be made between 'an internal consent' to particular judgments by him and obedience to his decisions as a matter of discipline rather than of doctrine.[54]

Throughout his Catholic period Newman continued to hold a balance between deference to authority and an openness to new ideas and developments. Thus at the very end of his life, with regard to the increasingly vexed problem of the Bible and science, he urged: 'Surely it becomes us to imitate the Church's patience, not rudely to attempt to force the hand of authority, but to _prepare the way_ for a final decision _by collecting points_ which may or may not be taken up in it.'[55] As we shall see, the importance of both patience and of the theological preparation needed for developments in church teaching were themes at the heart of Newman's idea of the Church.

Again, at the end of his life when he was nearly 80, he wrote in a private letter that 'I . . . am as fierce in my heart now as ever against Liberalism on the one hand and . . . extreme views . . . on the other.'[56] The 'extreme' views referred to, of course, were those of Ultramontane or integralist Catholics. This Catholic _via media_ Newman stated in print when he took over the editorship of the _Rambler_ in 1859, declaring that he intended to continue the same policy as before – 'to combine devotion to the Church with discrimination and candour in the treatment of her opponents; to reconcile freedom of thought with implicit faith;

[53] _LD_ xviii. 560.
[54] _LD_ xx. 331.
[55] _LD_ xxxi. 220.
[56] _LD_ xxviii. 207.

to discountenance what is untenable and unreal, without forgetting the tenderness due to the weak and the reverence rightly claimed for what is sacred; and to encourage a manly investigation of subjects of public interest under a deep sense of the prerogatives of ecclesiastical authority'. At the time Newman knew very well that he would be caught 'between two fires'.[57] But he also knew how important it was to have a forum like the *Rambler* for educated Catholics, if only because where 'education is widely promoted, and thought in consequence is active and incessant, it is a great thing to have a safety-valve, lest in particular minds there should be a formidable generation of steam and an explosion'.[58] But where there was a direct conflict between authority and freedom, Newman was in no doubt that the former held the field (except, of course, as we shall see, where moral considerations dictated otherwise). It might be 'tyrannical' to interfere in the freedom of the *Rambler,* but authority had 'the right' and 'a man who opposes legitimate authority is in a false position'. It was not 'courage', in his view, 'to run counter to constituted superiors – *they* bear the responsibility and to them we must leave it'.[59]

This deference to authority never left Newman, even at the height of the Ultramontane persecution of himself and the moderate liberal Catholicism he stood for. For example, he forthrightly dismissed any so-called ecumenical attempts to make the papacy more acceptable by limiting its powers:

> there is no use in a Pope at all, except to bind the whole of Christendom into one polity; and . . . to ask us to give up his universal jurisdiction is to invite us to commit suicide . . . An honorary head . . . does not affect the real force, or enter into the essence, of a political body, and is not worth contending about. We do not want a man of straw, but a bond of unity . . . Now the Church is a Church Militant, and, as the commander of an army is despotic, so must the visible head of the Church be . . .[60]

Since it is a part of Newman's rhetorical strategy to express the particular aspect or point of view he wants to emphasise in as

[57] *LD* xix. 88, 90.
[58] *LD* xix. 530.
[59] *LD* xix. 523.
[60] *LD* xxiii. 106.

extreme terms as possible, there may be, are likely to, be other complementary or even conflicting facets of the same question that also need stressing, and which Newman (as we shall see) will highlight with the same vigour. So here in this passage he is not intending to deny the rights of the episcopate or theologians or the laity, but he does mean to concentrate the mind on what in practice a focus of unity has to be if it is in fact to be a means of real unity, that is to say a central authority which can take decisions that are binding. Since Vatican II there have been many voices advocating such a devolution of power as to make the pope little more than an Archbishop of Canterbury, whose merely honorary primacy has failed to prevent the disintegration of the Anglican Communion and the effective loss of communion between various autonomous provinces. Nobody deplored Roman authoritarianism more than Newman; but nobody too saw more clearly that for unity the Church needs a head who has authority, and if necessary an authority with real cutting edge. No pope can impose alien beliefs on the Church; a pope who attempted to do so would be a heretic who thereby ceased to be pope, St. Thomas Aquinas held. But the Church on earth has to have a final source of authority if she is to remain true to her ultimate source of identity, Christ himself. The most conciliarist Catholic has to admit that someone has to call a council of the Church, someone has to preside over it, and someone has to confirm its decisions as those of an authentic council. Just as every national state needs a head to retain its identity and unity, so too the Church, to preserve its essential oneness, must have a head who more than merely chairs or coordinates the other bishops. Otherwise, there may be the outward appearance of unity, but the reality will certainly be disunity. From this point of view Newman was no liberal, but rather in the original sense of the word an 'ultramontane' Catholic, that is to say a Catholic who believes that for the local church to continue as both a free and integral part of the universal Church it is vital that there should be a supreme bishop 'beyond the Alps' with power to intervene.

Newman's conviction about the vital need for a strong, independent papacy did not, however, involve any diminution of his no less firmly held conviction that it was important that there should be a large degree of freedom and tolerance in the Church. Although there might be exceptions (as we shall see), his view was that new ideas should be given a generous airing:

> You may stifle them; or you may refuse them elbow-room; or again you may torment them with your continuing meddling; or you may let them have free course and range, and be content, instead of anticipating their excesses, to expose and restrain those excesses after they have occurred. But you have only this alternative; and for myself, I prefer much wherever it is possible, to be first generous and then just; to grant full liberty of thought, and to call it to account when abused.[61]

In contrast to the 'tyranny and terrorism' of the Ultramontane party, that 'formidable conspiracy, which is in action against the theological liberty of Catholics', he could not 'endure narrrowing the terms of Catholicity, as some would narrow them'. His own cherished maxim was 'In necessariis unitas, in dubiis libertas, in omnibus charitas' (in essentials unity, in doubtful matters liberty, in all things charity).[62] They were words which Pope John XXIII was to use in his opening address at the Second Vatican Council, which he had called to try and restore Christian unity and to renew the Catholic Church in the modern world. By this time Ultramontane extremism had had great success in 'inculcating as necessary to be believed what is not necessary, circumscribing the allowable liberty of the mind, at making certain political views as virtually de fide, at tying down Catholic action to what is obsolete and effete, and thereby at unsettling the faith of Catholic youth and talent, and making a dreadful breach between society and religion'.[63]

In order to be as precise as possible about the extent and nature of Newman's liberal Catholicism, it is worth looking in some detail at the three key issues to which he made an important theological contribution. The first is the relation between authority and freedom or between the magisterium and the theologians; the second the meaning of the doctrine of papal infallibility; and the third the rights and duties of the individual conscience. All three are obviously still burning topics and

[61] *Diff.* ii. 79.
[62] *LD* xxiii. 187, 189–90.
[63] *LD* xxiv. 247–8.

naturally range conservative against liberal Catholics. The way in which Newman mediates between the extreme positions in each case reveals very clearly the sense in which he may and the sense in which he may not be called a liberal Catholic.

The brilliant exposition of a balanced tension between authority and theology that is to be found in the last great chapter of the *Apologia* is foreshadowed, as so often, in Newman's private correspondence. Thus in 1863, discussing the question of intellectual freedom in the Church, he asks: 'Why was it that the Medieval Schools were so vigorous? because they were allowed free and fair play – because the disputants were not made to feel the bit in their mouths at every other word they spoke, but could move their limbs freely; and expatiate at will.' Not that the importance of authority is in any way rejected, but rather it is, he suggests, in the creative interplay between the magisterium and private judgment that truth is attained: 'when they went wrong, a stronger and truer intellect set them down – and, as time went on, if the dispute got perilous, and a controversialist obstinate, then at length Rome interfered – at length, not at first – Truth is wrought out by many minds, working together freely.' It is in these exploratory letters that we see a vigorously independent and original mind, yet one imbued with a profound sense of authority and tradition, in the actual process of forming a balanced theory of the teaching office of the Church. And, as always with Newman, theory is built on history: 'As far as I can make out, this has ever been the rule of the Church till now, when the first French Revolution having destroyed the Schools of Europe, a sort of centralisation has been established at headquarters – and the individual thinker . . . is brought into immediate collision with the most sacred authorities of the Divine Polity.'[64] This centralising process had, of course, been greatly accelerated by the rise and triumph of Ultramontanism.

Against the extreme Ultramontanes Newman insists in a letter to a potential convert on the limits of what somebody has to believe in order to become a Catholic:

> To submit to the Church means this, first that you will receive as de fide whatever she proposes de fide; that you will submit to

[64] *LD* xx. 425–6.

the decisions of Schola Theologorum, when unanimous in matters of faith and morals, as being so sure that it is forbidden to contradict them – that you obey the commands of the Church in act and deed, though as a matter of policy prudence etc. you may think that other commands would be better. You are not called on to believe de fide any thing but what has been promulgated as such – You are not called on to excuse an internal belief of any doctrine which Sacred Congregations, Local Synods, or particular Bishops, or the Pope as a private Doctor, may enunciate. You are not called upon ever to believe or act against the moral law, at the command of any superior.[65]

This succinctly comprehensive statement keeps a careful balance between conservative and liberal approaches to the authority of the Church. On the one hand only those doctrines which are manifestly articles of faith actually require belief, while no order from any superior is to be obeyed if it is against one's conscience. On the other hand, a 'submission', as Newman puts it, is required to the Catholic tradition in faith and morals as the theologians expound it, as well as obedience to the laws and precepts of the Church. The central problem for modern Catholics, it is true, is not even touched on as Newman did not foresee the stream of authoritative but non-infallible papal teachings that advances in medicine and psychology would cause in the area of sexuality in the 20th century. However, as we shall see, his teaching on conscience does have an important bearing on this difficult area.

But before considering conscience, it is time to turn to the last great chapter of the *Apologia,* which is one of Newman's finest pieces of writing and where he carefully balances the rights of the individual, particularly the theologian, and those of church authority.[66] His starting point is a defence of the infallibility of the Church. Granted that 'truth is the real object of our reason', then 'right reason' when 'correctly exercised' arrives at religious truth. But unfortunately, 'reason as it acts in fact and concretely in fallen man' has a 'tendency . . . towards simple unbelief', and there is no denying 'the all-corroding, all-dissolving scepticism of the intellect', which has resulted in an 'anarchical condition of

[65] *LD* xx. 545.
[66] For the following discussion see Ker, *Newman on Being a Christian,* 87–103.

things'. Just as 'in the pagan world, when our Lord came, the last traces of the religious knowledge of former times were all but disappearing from those portions of the world in which the intellect had been active and had had a career', so too, in the modern world, 'What a scene, what a prospect, does the whole of Europe present at this day!' The necessity 'to arrest fierce wilful human nature in its onward course' in order to preserve 'some form of religion for the interests of humanity' led to the establishment of religion at the Reformation in Protestant countries, 'but now the crevices of those establishments are admitting the enemy'; nor can the Bible as 'a book . . . make a stand against the wild living intellect of man'. The conflict between the claims of reason and religion is resolved through 'the Church's infallibility, as a provision, adapted by the mercy of the Creator, to preserve religion in the world, and to restrain that freedom of thought, which of course in itself is one of the greatest of our natural gifts, and to rescue it from its own suicidal excesses'. This 'power . . . is happily adapted to be a working instrument . . . for smiting hard and throwing back the immense energy of the aggressive, capricious, untrustworthy intellect.'[67]

There follows a severely uncompromising exposition of the Church's authority 'viewed in its fullness' and 'viewed in the concrete, as clothed and surrounded by the appendages of its high sovereignty . . . a supereminent prodigious power sent upon earth to encounter and master a giant evil'. Although infallibility strictly only belongs to solemn dogmatic definitions, Newman professes to submit not only to the traditions of the Church, but also 'to those other decisions of the Holy See, theological or not . . . which, waiving the question of their infallibility, on the lowest ground come to me with a claim to be accepted and obeyed'. Nor does he feel any 'temptation at all to break in pieces the great legacy of thought' which the Church has inherited from its greatest thinkers. This raises the obvious objection that 'the restless intellect of our common humanity is utterly weighed down' by such an authority, 'so that, if this is to be the mode of bringing it into order, it is brought into order

[67] *Apo.* 218–20.

only to be destroyed'. Newman's reply is that in fact the 'energy of the human intellect . . . thrives and is joyous, with a tough elastic strength, under the terrible blows of the divinely-fashioned weapon, and is never so much itself as when it has lately been overthrown'. And he argues that far from being mutually contradictory, authority and reason need each other precisely because, paradoxically, each is actually sustained by conflict with the other:

> It is the vast Catholic body itself, and it only, which affords an arena for both combatants in that awful, never-dying duel. It is necessary for the very life of religion . . . that the warfare should be incessantly carried on. Every exercise of Infallibility is brought out into act by an intense and varied operation of the Reason, both as its ally and as its opponent, and provokes again, when it has done its work, a re-action of Reason against it; and, as in a civil polity the State exists and endures by means of the rivalry and collision, the encroachments and defeats of its constituent parts, so in like manner Catholic Christendom is no simple exhibition of religious absolutism, but presents a continuous picture of Authority and Private Judgment alternately advancing and retreating as the ebb and flow of the tide; – it is a vast assemblage of human beings with wilful intellects and wild passions, brought together into one by the beauty and the Majesty of a Superhuman Power, – into what may be called a large reformatory or training-school, not as if into a hospital or into a prison, not in order to be sent to bed, not to be buried alive, but (if I may change my metaphor) brought together as if into some moral factory, for the melting, refining and moulding, by an incessant, noisy process, of the raw material of human nature, so excellent, so dangerous, so capable of divine purposes.[68]

The startling chain of imagery that concludes this richly metaphorical passage hints at a new, divergent movement of argument, and reminds us that Newman also has readers other than Protestants or unbelievers in mind. The infallible authority, he insists with a typically secular metaphor, 'is a supply for a need, and it does not go beyond that need', for its purpose is 'not to enfeeble the freedom or vigour of human thought in

[68] *Apo.* 224–6.

religious speculation, but to resist and control its extravagance'. Having begun by freely admitting the wide powers enjoyed by ecclesiastical authority, he now emphasises both the narrow limits of infallibility in defining as explicit doctrine what is already implicit in revelation, and also its rare occurrence (normally by a 'Pope in Ecumenical Council'). But, more important, he recognises what '*is* the great trial to the Reason', namely, that the Church claims jurisdiction over a wide area of 'secular matters which bear upon religion'. These disciplinary rather than doctrinal judgments are not, however, infallible; nevertheless, they claim obedience (but not faith). Again, 'because there is a gift of infallibility in the Catholic Church', it does not necessarily follow that 'the parties who are in possession of it are in all their proceedings infallible'. Indeed, 'I think history supplies us with instances in the Church, where legitimate power has been harshly used.' The unequivocal assertion of the Church's legitimate authority is thus sharply qualified by these reminders of its limits and restraints. But the apparent discrepancy is resolved by the consideration that it does not 'follow that the substance of the acts of the ruling power is not right and expedient, because its manner may have been faulty'. In fact, Newman remarks tartly, 'high authorities act by means of instruments', and 'we know how such instruments claim for themselves the name of their principals, who thus get the credit of faults which really are not theirs'.[69]

The pages that follow are probably unrivalled in Newman's works for their sharply antithetical style of argument, brilliantly deployed to hold a carefully poised balance between two diametrically opposed points of view. But the object is not to play a mere balancing trick between conservative Catholics on the one side and liberal Catholics on the other. Nor is the pattern of thought no more than a rhetorical device designed to reach a compromise between the claims of both parties. For what emerges is that truth is attained not in spite of but through the conflict of opposites, which forces the crucial shift of perspective that allows the dilemma to be seen in a new light and so to be resolved.

[69] *Apo.* 226, 229–31.

Newman begins by reinforcing the case for authority and the need for submission. Even Protestants 'have before now obeyed the royal command to abstain from certain theological questions'. Moreover, despite all abuses, Newman insists that ecclesiastical authority has been 'mainly in the right'. For example, Origen 'was wrong' and 'his opponents were right'. And yet 'who can speak with patience of his enemy and the enemy of St. John Chrysostom, that Theophilus, bishop of Alexandria? who can admire or revere Pope Vigilius?' The contradiction is resolved by a completely fresh perspective, at once enlightening and provocative:

> In reading ecclesiastical history, when I was an Anglican, it used to be forcibly brought home to me, how the initial error of what afterwards became heresy was the urging forward of some truth against the prohibition of authority at an unseasonable time. There is a time for every thing, and many a man desires a reformation of an abuse, or the fuller development of a doctrine, or the adoption of a particular policy, but forgets to ask himself whether the right time for it is come: and knowing that there is no one who will be doing any thing towards its accomplishment in his own lifetime unless he does it himself, he will not listen to the voice of authority, and he spoils a good work in his own century, in order that another man, as yet unborn, may not have the opportunity of bringing it happily to perfection in the next. He may seem to the world to be nothing else than a bold champion for the truth and a martyr to free opinion, when he is just one of those persons whom the competent authority ought to silence; and, though the case may not fall within that subject-matter in which that authority is infallible, or the formal conditions of the exercise of that gift may be wanting, it is clearly the duty of authority to act vigorously in the case.

This, Newman admits, will arouse criticism, especially 'if the ruling power happens in its proceedings to evince any defect of prudence or consideration'. Mindful, no doubt, of his own difficulties with liberal Catholics who disliked his insistence on obedience, Newman adds that 'all those who take the part of that ruling authority will be considered as time-servers, or indifferent to the cause of uprightness and truth'. But that is not the conclusion of the sentence. The surprise, or rather the sting, lies in the second half, directed not at the liberals, but at the

Ultramontanes: 'while, on the other hand, the said authority may be accidentally supported by a violent ultra party, which exalts opinions into dogmas, and has it principally at heart to destroy every school of thought but its own'.

This 'state of things' may well provoke and discourage people of moderate views, as well as 'such as keenly perceive, and are honestly eager to remedy, existing evils' – 'evils', Newman comments acidly, 'of which divines in this or that foreign country know nothing at all, and which even at home, where they exist, it is not every one who has the means of estimating'. The bewildering progress in modern knowledge raises the critical question, 'how are the respective claims of revelation and of natural science to be adjusted?' particularly out of 'tenderness for those many souls who, in consequence of the confident tone of the schools of secular knowledge, are in danger of being led away into a bottomless liberalism of thought'. This 'deep, plausible scepticism', which is 'the development of human reason, as practically exercised by the natural man', now constitutes 'the educated lay world'. However, Newman is not intent on attacking the 'Liberal religionists of this day' ('a very mixed body') or contemporary scientists and scholars, some of whom may be hostile to religion, but many of whom pursue their research in a completely disinterested spirit and should not be blamed (as if one 'were afraid of truth of any kind') for pursuing 'secular facts, by means of the reason which God has given them, to their logical conclusions'. Rather, he is concerned for those educated believers 'who are simply perplexed, – frightened or rendered desperate . . . by the utter confusion into which late discoveries or speculations have thrown their most elementary ideas of religion'.

Beneath the warm compassion runs a cold undercurrent of contempt for the heartlessness of obscurantist dogmatism:

> Who does not feel for such men? who can have one unkind thought of them? Let them be fierce with you who have no experience of the difficulty with which error is discriminated from truth, and the way of life is found amid the illusions of the world.

'How many a Catholic,' exclaims Newman, 'has in his thoughts followed such men, many of them so good, so true, so noble! how often has the wish risen in his heart that some one from among his own people should come forward as the champion of revealed truth against its opponents!' Indeed, he has himself been asked to do so by both Catholics and Protestants. But he raises a serious objection: 'at the moment it is so difficult to say precisely what it is that is to be encountered and overthrown ... hypotheses rise and fall'. It is so 'difficult to anticipate which of them will keep their ground' that 'it has seemed to me to be very undignified for a Catholic to commit himself to the work of chasing what might turn out to be phantoms'. Nor would such an attempt be likely to find favour with the authorities of the Church, whose 'recent acts' may be interpreted, Newman suggest politely, as 'tying the hands of a controversialist ... and teaching us that true wisdom, which Moses inculcated on his people, when the Egyptians were pursuing them, "Fear ye not, stand still; the Lord shall fight for you, and ye shall hold your peace"'. He concludes, therefore: 'And so far from finding a difficulty in obeying in this case, I have cause to be thankful and to rejoice to have so clear a direction in a matter of difficulty.'

In reality, Newman argues, there has never in the past been any conflict between religion and science. But immediately he qualifies the point both by admitting that it is too soon to pronounce on the relation between modern science and theology, and by freely conceding the one notorious exception to the rule, the case of Galileo. With this ambivalent allusion, the anti-Ultramontane undercurrent begins to swell to an undertow, stronger than the ostensible drift of the argument against objections to an infallible authority. The proof, Newman continues, that infallibility has not crushed intellectual freedom in the Church is that it is 'individuals, and not the Holy See, that have taken the initiative, and given the lead to the Catholic mind, in theological inquiry'. 'Indeed,' he points out, 'it is one of the reproaches against the Roman Church, that it has originated nothing, and has only served as a sort of *remora* or break in the development of doctrine. And it is an objection which I really embrace as a truth; for such I conceive to be the main purpose of its extraordinary gift.'

The historical examples that follow are unrelentingly negative. The fact is that 'the Church of Rome possessed no great mind in the whole period of persecution'. There was not a single Doctor till St. Leo, who anyway taught only 'one point of doctrine'. Not even Pope St. Gregory has a place in the history of theology. The greatest Western theologian, St. Augustine, belonged, like the best early Latin theologians, to the African Church. Western theology, in fact, was formed to a considerable extent by heterodox theologians such as Tertullian and Origen and Eusebius, with the result that actual heretical 'questionings' became 'salutary truths'. Even ecumenical councils were guided by the 'individual reason' of a mere presbyter like Malchion, or a young deacon like Athanasius. At Trent, too, particular theologians 'had a critical effect on some of the definitions of dogma'. The real, albeit hidden, conclusion is that history gives little support to the Ultramontane view of Rome as a kind of oracle of truth.

History, too, shows how little authority has interfered with the freedom of theologians. But Newman is not only protesting against the present by means of the past; he is also stating with great deliberateness his considered view on the crucial balance to be maintained between theology and the teaching authority of the Church. He begins by referring (provocatively) to that medieval theocratic society so idealised by many of his contemporaries:

> There never was a time when the intellect of the educated class was more active, or rather more restless, than in the middle ages. And then again all through Church history from the first, how slow is authority in interfering! Perhaps a local teacher, or a doctor in some local school, hazards a proposition, and a controversy ensues. It smoulders or burns in one place, no one interposing; Rome simply lets it alone. Then it comes before a Bishop; or some priest, or some professor in some other seat of learning takes it up; and then there is a second stage of it. Then it comes before a University, and it may be condemned by the theological faculty. So the controversy proceeds year after year, and Rome is still silent. An appeal perhaps is next made to a seat of authority inferior to Rome; and then at last after a long while it comes before the supreme power. Meanwhile, the question has been ventilated and turned over and over again, and viewed on every side of it, and authority is called upon to pronounce a decision, which has already been arrived at by reason. But even

then, perhaps the supreme authority hesitates to do so, and nothing is determined on the point for years; or so generally and vaguely, that the whole controversy has to be gone through again, before it is ultimately determined.

Newman refrains from outright criticism of the abuse of authority in the contemporary Church. But his point is clear enough.

> It is manifest how a mode of proceeding, such as this, tends not only to the liberty, but to the courage, of the individual theologian or controversialist. Many a man has ideas, which he hope are true, and useful for his day, but he is not confident about them, and wishes to have them discussed. He is willing, or rather would be thankful, to give them up, if they can be proved to be erroneous or dangerous, and by means of controversy he achieves his end. He is answered, and he yields; or on the contrary he finds that he is considered safe. He would not dare to do this, if he knew an authority, which was supreme and final, was watching every word he said, and made signs of assent or dissent to each sentence, as he uttered it. Then indeed he would be fighting, as the Persian soldiers, under the lash, and the freedom of his intellect might truly be said to be beaten out of him.

Nevertheless, he is ready to undermine his own indignation with the frank qualification that 'when controversies run high' then 'an interposition may . . . advisably take place; and again, questions may be of that urgent nature, that an appeal must, as a matter of duty, be made at once to the highest authority in the Church'.

But the insistent emphasis on the universal character of the Church that follows barely conceals an unfavourable allusion to the Italian monopoly of the Holy See.

> The multitude of nations which are within the fold of the Church will be found to have acted for its protection, against any narrowness, on the supposition of narrowness, in the various authorities at Rome, with whom lies the practical decision of controverted questions . . . Then, again, such national influences have a providential effect in moderating the bias which the local influences of Italy may exert on the See of St. Peter. It stands to reason that . . . Rome must have in it an element of Italy; and it is no prejudice to the zeal and devotion with which we submit

ourselves to the Holy See to admit this plainly . . . Catholicity is not only one of the notes of the Church, but . . . one of its securities.

And the conclusion is uncompromising:

I trust that all European races will ever have a place in the Church, and assuredly I think that the loss of the English, not to say the German element, in its composition has been a most serious misfortune. And certainly, if there is one consideration more than another which should make us English grateful to Pius the Ninth, it is that, by giving us a Church of our own, he has prepared the way for our own habits of mind, our own manner of reasoning, our own tastes, and our own virtues, finding a place and thereby a sanctification, in the Catholic Church.[70]

Since the Second Vatican Council, these hopes of Newman have, of course, been realised in the election of the first non-Italian Pope for several centuries, in the increasingly international character of the Roman curia, and in the new importance given to the local church. But while the council emphasised the importance of theologians, there are still many unresolved problems concerning their relationship to the magisterium or teaching authority of the Church. Newman's ecclesiology in this area is valuable not only for the balance it strikes between the interests of both sides, but also in two other respects. First, his evenhanded approach still strikes a very original note in its insistence on the positive fruits of a conflict that is as inevitable as it is potentially creative. Second, the mere fact that Newman has no blueprint to offer to resolve these tensions is itself significant in indicating that there are no simple solutions to problems which no more admit of a theoretical answer than does life itself. But I hope I have said enough to show how far Newman is from any simplistic conservatism or liberalism.

Newman had no difficulty, as we have seen, in accepting the First Vatican Council's definition of papal infallibility, which was more moderate and restrained than the kind of definition for which the extreme Ultramontanes had been agitating. Before the

[70] *Apo.* 231–41.

actual definition was passed, he pointed out in a private letter that however infallible the Pope might be, his pronouncements would still require interpretation. The same was true of a council's definitions, which – just as 'lawyers explain acts of Parliament' – had to be explained by theologians. Obvious as the fact might be, the conclusion to be drawn from it had serious consequences for the fantasies of extreme Ultramontanism: 'Hence, I have never been able to see myself that the ultimate decision rests with any but the general Catholic intelligence'.[71] However, later in *A Letter to the Duke of Norfolk* (1875) he was careful to emphasise that he simply meant that the whole Church ratified a definition as 'authentic', not that the 'subsequent reception' actually entered into the 'necessary conditions' of a dogmatic decision.[72] Thus, for example, the only answer in the last analysis to that tiny handful of schismatics who refuse to recognise the Second Vatican Council as an authentic general Council of the Church freely presided over by a legitimate Pope, is that the universal Church in fact recognises the Council as genuine and therefore binding. However, the fact that the Council Fathers did not first seek the approval or permission of the Church at large before coming to their decisions does not in any way detract from the validity of the proceedings.

In the earlier private letter Newman also noted that abstract definitions could not 'determine particular fact': the doctrine, for example, that there was no salvation outside the Church did not apply to people in 'invincible ignorance'.[73] For 'it does not follow, because there is no Church but one, which has the Evangelical gifts and privileges to bestow, that therefore no one can be saved without the intervention of that one Church'. And it was 'possible to belong to the soul of the Church without belonging to the body'. Other teachings of the Church admitted of exceptions in practice, like the condemnations in theory of interdenominational education and usury. In the case of usury, moreover, as in that of the doctrine of absolute predestination, distinctions had been drawn between different connotations of

[71] *LD* xxv. 71.
[72] *Diff.* ii. 372.
[73] *LD* xxv. 71.

the words in question, which had led to the serious modification, even suspension, of the abstract teaching. Such changes and qualifications in the Church's official teaching 'show what caution is to be observed' in interpreting its pronouncements. So much for any kind of Catholic fundamentalism or positivism. But, on the other hand, because general doctrines cannot be divorced from concrete circumstances and contexts, it did not follow that condemnations of 'the very wording' of particular doctrinal deviations in books may not be infallible, since otherwise 'neither Pope nor Council could draw up a dogmatic definition at all, for the right exercise of words is involved in the right exercise of thought'.[74]

He continued to insist after the definition that 'the voice of the Schola Theologorum, of the whole Church diffusive' would 'in time make itself heard', and that 'Catholic instincts and ideas' would eventually 'assimilate and harmonise' it with the wider context of Catholic belief.[75] As time went on, too, theologians would 'settle the force of the wording of the dogma, just as the courts of law solve the meaning and bearing of Acts of Parliament'.[76] It was hardly more than common sense that ultimately the solemn declarations of councils and popes could be authenticated only by the acceptance and recognition by the Church that the pronouncements were indeed what they purported to be; nevertheless, their interpretation involved necessarily the technicalities of theological science. The meaning of dogmatic statements was not self-evident, but they were 'always made with the anticipation and condition of this lawyer-like, or special-pleader-like, action of the intellect upon them'.[77] All human statements required interpretation. In defining doctrines, popes and councils enjoyed an 'active infallibility', but more was involved in the infallibility of the Church than that, since a *passive infallibility* belonged to the whole Catholic people, who had to determine the force and meaning of these

[74] *Diff.* ii. 335, 337, 330.
[75] *LD* xxv. 284.
[76] *LD* xxv. 447.
[77] *LD* xxvi. 35.

doctrinal definitions; the chief responsibility for this, however, lay with the theologians, whose discussions and investigations assured a clear distinction, essential for preventing 'dogmatism', between 'theological truth' and 'theological opinion'. Differences between theologians maintained 'liberty of thought', while their consensus on points of dogma was 'the safeguard of the infallible decisions of the Church'.[78] Infallibility (itself a comparatively recent term) resided in its fullness in the whole Church (although this had always been assumed and never formally defined).

Newman repeats and develops in *A Letter to the Duke of Norfolk* the points he had already made in private correspondence. He does not hesitate to say that the 'definite rules' and 'traditional principles of interpretation' needed for explaining dogmatic statements are 'as cogent and unchangeable' as the definitions themselves.[79] Central to this process, he claims, is the 'principle of minimising',[80] whereby theologians construe 'in the concrete' a pronouncement of the teaching authority, 'by strict interpretation of its wording, by the illustration of its circumstances, and by the recognition of exceptions, in order to make it as tolerable as possible, and the least of a temptation, to self-willed, independent, or wrongly educated minds'. After all, he insists, the virtue of faith is 'so difficult', and 'so difficult is it to assent inwardly to propositions, verified to us neither by reason nor experience, but depending for their reception on the word of the Church as God's oracle, that she has ever shown the utmost care to contract, as far as possible, the range of truths and the sense of propositions, of which she demands this absolute reception'.[81] This 'legitimate minimising' takes advantage on the one hand of the 'intensely concrete character of the matters condemned' in 'negative' pronouncements, and on the other hand of the abstract nature of 'affirmative' definitions of doctrine ('excepting such as relate to persons'), which 'admit of exceptions in their actual application'.[82] These

[78] *LD* xxvii. 338.
[79] *Diff.* ii. 280.
[80] *Diff.* ii. 332
[81] *Diff.* ii. 320–1.
[82] *Diff.* ii. 334.

principles have to be applied to the definition of papal infallibility, the scope of which is carefully limited to deliberate and actual definitions of faith and morals that are referable either to revelation or to the moral law, and that are intended to be authoritative teachings, binding on the whole Church as pertaining to salvation. In the event, however, of 'a false interpretation' of the definition of infallibility, then 'another Leo will be given us for the occasion'. The reference is to Pope St. Leo's Council of Chalcedon, which, 'without of course touching the definition' of the preceding Council of Ephesus, 'trimmed the balance of doctrine by completing it'.[83] The warning is an exact prophecy both of the theology of 'creeping infallibility' that came in the wake of the First Vatican Council, and of the Second Vatican Council, which Pope John XXIII convoked nearly a hundred years later.

At the heart of *A Letter to the Duke of Norfolk* is the celebrated treatment of the sovereignty of conscience. Newman had often written on conscience as the basis of religious belief, but here he discusses the individual believer's conscience in its relation to legitimate ecclesiastical authority. He first defines conscience as the law of God 'as apprehended in the minds of individual men' – which, 'though it may suffer refraction in passing into the intellectual medium of each . . . is not therefore so affected as to lose its character of being the Divine Law, but still has, as such, the prerogative of commanding obedience'. On this view, conscience is 'the voice of God', whereas the world regards it as little more than 'a creation of man'. Far from being 'a long-sighted selfishness' or 'a desire to be consistent with oneself', Newman declares in ringing tones, 'Conscience is the aboriginal Vicar of Christ, a prophet in its information, a monarch in its peremptoriness, a priest in its blessings and anathemas, and, even though the eternal priesthood throughout the Church could cease to be, in it the sacerdotal principle would remain and would have a sway.'

In earlier times 'its supremacy was assailed by the arm of physical force', but 'now the intellect is put in operation to sap the foundations of a power which the sword could not destroy'.

---

[83] *Diff.* ii. 307.

The threat is grandiloquently conveyed, but for all its fragile vulnerability, conscience has a strange, indestructible life:

> All through my day there has been a resolute warfare, I had almost said conspiracy against the rights of conscience, as I have described it. Literature and science have been embodied in great institutions in order to put it down. Noble buildings have been reared as fortresses against the spiritual, invisible influence which is too subtle for science and too profound for literature. Chairs in Universities have been made the seats of an antagonist tradition.

The secularised idea of conscience merely concerns 'the right of thinking, speaking, writing, and acting' as one sees fit, 'without any thought of God at all'. Paradoxically, it has become 'the very right and freedom of conscience to dispense with conscience'. In effect, conscience 'has been superseded by a counterfeit', namely, 'the right of self-will'.[84] Thus Newman rejects any secular liberal concept of conscience.

Were, however, the pope himself to 'speak against Conscience in the true sense of the word, he would commit a suicidal act. He would be cutting the ground from under his feet.' Indeed, continues Newman, 'we shall find that it is by the universal sense of right and wrong, the consciousness of transgression, the pangs of guilt, and the dread of retribution, as first principles deeply lodged in the hearts of men, it is thus and only thus, that he has gained his footing in the world and achieved his success'. The 'championship of the Moral Law and of conscience' is 'his *raison d'etre*', and the 'fact of his mission is the answer to the complaints of those who feel the insufficiency of the natural light; and the insufficiency of that light is the justification of his mission'. Once again Newman emphasises the precarious nature of the moral sense, which 'is at once the highest of all teachers, yet the least luminous; and the Church, the Pope, the Hierarchy are . . . the supply of an urgent demand'. But if revelation is the fulfilment of natural religion, it is in no sense 'independent of it': 'The Pope, who comes of Revelation, has no jurisdiction over Nature.'[85]

---

[84] *Diff.* ii. 247–50
[85] *Diff.* ii. 252–4

Turning to the crucial question of the relation of individual conscience to authority, Newman begins by laying down the principle that since 'conscience is not a judgment upon any speculative truth, any abstract doctrine, but bears immediately . . . on something to be done or not done', it 'cannot come into direct collision with the Church's or the Pope's infallibility; which is engaged on general propositions, and in the condemnation of particular and given errors'. Here Newman means by conscience not what moral theologians call *habitual* conscience, that is, conscience as it adheres to general moral norms and principles, but rather what they mean by *actual* conscience, that is, the judgment that this particular act here and now is to be done or not done as falling or not falling under the relevant moral precept. For example, my habitual conscience tells me that torturing children is wrong, but my actual conscience has to decide whether this particular punishment is or is not an act of torture. And so, Newman argues, because actual conscience is 'a practical dictate', direct conflict is possible 'only when the Pope legislates, or gives particular orders, and the like'. However, 'a Pope is not infallible in his laws, nor in his commands, nor in his acts of state, nor in his administration, nor in his public policy'. After all, St. Peter was not infallible at Antioch when St. Paul disagreed with him nor was Liberius when he excommunicated Athanasius.

However, the 'dictate' of conscience, 'in order to prevail against the voice of the Pope, must follow upon serious thought, prayer, and all available means of arriving at a right judgment on the matter in question'. The onus of proof, then, lies on the individual conscience: 'Unless a man is able to say to himself, as in the Presence of God, that he must not, and dare not, act upon the Papal injunction, he is bound to obey it, and would commit a great sin in disobeying it.'[86] As usual, Newman's bold admission about the fallibility of the first pope in no way excludes a rigorous emphasis on loyalty and obedience to a legitimate superior. On the other hand, to obey a papal order which one seriously thinks is wrong would be a sin – even if one is culpably mistaken (a person may be to blame for having a false

---

[86] *Diff.* ii. 256–8

conscience, but not for acting in accordance with it). In the last analysis, conscience, however misguided, is supreme, and Newman concludes the discussion calmly, even casually, with the famous declaration:

> I add one remark. Certainly, if I am obliged to bring religion into after-dinner toasts, (which indeed does not seem quite the thing) I shall drink – to the Pope, if you please – still, to Conscience first, and to the Pope afterwards.[87]

Newman's last contribution to ecclesiology or the theology of the Church is the classic Preface of 1877 to his new edition of *Lectures on the Prophetical Office of the Church* (1837). In it he placed a heavy emphasis on the importance of the theology:

> I say, then, Theology is the fundamental and regulating principle of the whole Church system. It is commensurate with Revelation, and the Revelation is the initial and essential idea of Christianity. It is the subject-matter, the formal cause, the expression, of the Prophetical Office, and, as being such, has created both the Regal Office and the Sacerdotal. And it has in a certain sense a power of jurisdiction over those offices, as being its own creations, theologians being ever in request and in employment in keeping within bounds both the political and popular elements in the Church's constitution . . .

But if Newman is no Catholic fundamentalist, he is certainly no theological liberal either. Far from thinking that it is the theologians who should run the Church, he asserts unequivocally: 'Yet theology cannot always have its own way; it is too hard, too intellectual, too exact, to be always equitable, or to be always compassionate . . .' Sometimes even a theologian in his writings has to 'let his devout nature betray itself between the joints of his theological harness'. Popular religion may, for example, reject a more accurate translation of the Bible because to 'the devotional mind what is new and strange is as repulsive, often as dangerous, as falsehood is to the scientific. Novelty is often error to those who are unprepared for it, from the refraction with which it enters into their conceptions.' However wrong the condemnation of Galileo, nevertheless

---

[87] *Diff.* ii. 261.

there was nothing wrong in censuring abrupt, startling, unsettling, unverified disclosures ... at once uncalled for and inopportune, at a time when the limits of revealed truth had not as yet been ascertained. A man ought to be very sure of what he is saying, before he risks the chance of contradicting the word of God. It was safe, not dishonest, to be slow in accepting what nevertheless turned out to be true. Here is an instance in which the Church obliges Scripture expositors, at a given time or place, to be tender of the popular religious sense.

People's 'imaginations' have to become accustomed to religious changes, whereas 'when science crosses and breaks the received path of Revelation', religious people are criticised if 'they show hesitation to shift at a minute's warning their position, and to accept as truths shadowy views at variance with what they have ever been taught and have held'. The modern idea is that it is 'a great moral virtue to be fearless and thorough in inquiry into facts', whereas the 'pursuit of truth in the subject-matter of religion ... must always be accompanied by the fear of error'.[88] Elsewhere, Newman says: 'What the genius of the Church cannot bear is, changes in thought being hurried, abrupt, violent – out of tenderness to souls, for unlearned and narrow minded men get unsettled and miserable. The great thing is to move all together and then the change, as geological changes, must be very slow.' And yet, on the other hand, in another letter, he insists on the role of theology in preparing the Church for changes – 'it is the arena on which questions of development and change are argued out ... it prepares the way, accustoming the mind of Catholics to the idea of the change'. Because theology also, he explains in the same letter, 'protects' dogma by 'forming a large body of doctrine which must be got through before an attack can be made on the dogma', without theology 'the dogma of the Church would be the raw flesh without skin – nay or a tree without leaves – for, as devotional feelings clothe the dogma on the one hand, so does the teaching of [theology] on the other'.[89]

The Church allows much more freedom in devotion, which is 'of a subjective and personal nature', than in doctrine. This

[88] *VM* i. xlvii-l, lii-lvi.
[89] *LD* xxv. 31–2; xxii. 99.

contrast is accentuated if 'ecclesiastical authority takes part with popular sentiment against a theological decision'. A very early example would be the occasion at Antioch when St. Peter stopped associating with converts from paganism because of pressure from converts from Judaism, a lapse for which he was rebuked by St. Paul. However, Paul himself was ready to conform to Jewish customs when necessary, and the principle of 'accommodation' – though it may be misapplied, as perhaps in the case of the Jesuit missionaries' adoption of Chinese customs – has always been practised by Christians since the earliest time.[90]

The theological office of the Church, then, may find itself in opposition to both the so-called political and pastoral offices. And Newman does not hesitate to say that at times it will have to give way. In conclusion, therefore, we may say that if a deference to theological inquiry is of the essence of a liberal Christian, then to that extent Newman is a liberal. But where he is not a liberal is in asserting that the theological is not the only office of the Church and that at times it has to play a subordinate office. Once again we see that Newman eludes the usual categories of liberal and conservative.

[90] *VM* i. lxxv–lxxvi.

5

Eastern Christianity

When[1] Newman visited Greece on his Mediterranean tour of 1832–3, he wrote the poem called 'The Greek Fathers', which begins with the lines:

> Let heathens sing thy heathen praise,
> Fall'n Greece! the thought of holier days
>   In my sad heart abides;
> For sons of thine in Truth's first hour
> Were tongues and weapons of His power,
> Born of the Spirit's fiery shower,
>   Our fathers and our guides.[2]

When he later said, 'The Fathers made me a Catholic',[3] he was thinking particularly of the Greek or Eastern Fathers rather than the later Latin Western Fathers. As he never tired of saying, he became a Catholic because he became convinced that the early patristic Church and the contemporary Roman Catholic Church were the same Church, all outward appearances to the contrary. Before his conversion,

> I was asking myself what would the Fathers have done, what would those whose works were around my room, whose names were ever meeting my eyes, whose authority was ever influencing my judgment, what would those men have said, how would they have acted in my position?[4]

---

[1] I am greatly indebted in this chapter to Charles Stephen Dessain, 'Cardinal Newman and the Eastern Tradition', *The Downside Review*, 94 (April 1976), 83–98.

[2] *VV* 102.

[3] *Diff.* ii. 24.

[4] *Ess.* ii. 74.

And so as he wrote his *Essay on the Development of Christian Doctrine*, he became finally convinced of the truth of the claims of Rome, if only because it seemed all too obvious that the Fathers would · feel more at home in the modern Roman Catholic Church than in the Church of England:

> On the whole, all parties will agree that, of all existing systems, the present communion of Rome is the nearest approximation in fact to the Church of the Fathers, possible though some may think it, to be nearer still to that Church on paper. Did St. Athanasius or St. Ambrose come suddenly to life, it cannot be doubted what communion he would take to be his own.[5]

Conversion to the Church of Rome was a veritable coming home to the Church of the East:

> I recollect well what an outcast I seemed to myself, when I took down from the shelves of my library the volumes of St. Athanasius or St. Basil, and set myself to study them; and how, on the contrary, when at length I was brought into Catholic communion, I kissed them with delight, with a feeling that in them I had more than all that I had lost; and, as though I were directly addressing the glorious saints, who bequeathed them to the Church, how I said to the inanimate pages, 'You are now mine, and I am now yours, beyond any mistake.'[6]

The Eastern Father who most deeply influenced Newman's theology was St. Athanasius, but he was also much influenced by St. Basil, St. Gregory of Nyssa, St. Gregory Nazianzen, and St. Cyril of Alexandria. He was attracted too by the thought of St. Clement and of, Origen, 'whose broad philosophy,' he wrote, 'carried me away'.[7] It was this theology that shaped and guided Newman's reading of the Scriptures, out of which emerged that magnificent body of Anglican sermons that is one of the great classics of Christian spirituality. It is also obviously at the heart of Newman's Anglican theology, especially his *Lectures on the Doctrine of Justification* (1838). The fact that Newman's thought is so deeply scriptural and patristic recommends it in a special way to a revived Catholic theology that seeks to return to the sources of the tradition as well as to enter into ecumenical

[5] *Dev.* 97–8.
[6] *Diff.* ii. 3.
[7] *Apo.* 36.

dialogue with other Christians. However, it was an important reason, too, why his theology was regarded with suspicion in his own time by integralist Catholics who saw Western scholasticism as the exclusive theology of the Church. Thus in his *A Letter to Pusey* (1865), Newman admitted that his 'deference to Antiquity' would be regarded as 'a mistake' by some of his co-religionists. But, he maintained roundly,

> I am not ashamed still to take my stand upon the Fathers, and do not mean to budge. The history of their times is not yet an old almanac to me. Of course I maintain the value and authority of the 'Schola', as one of the *loci theologici*; nevertheless I sympathise with Petavius in preferring to the 'contentious and subtle theology' of the middle age, that 'more elegant and fruitful teaching which is moulded after the image of erudite Antiquity.' The Fathers made me a Catholic, and I am not gong to kick down the ladder by which I ascended into the Church.[8]

And again later in 1873 he told (privately) an Anglican correspondent that he did not expect his article on 'Causes of the Rise and Successes of Arianism',[9] in which he explained the Trinitarian theology of the Eastern Fathers, to 'please . . . even my own people'.[10]

The rationalism of Western theology has long been an object of criticism by the Eastern Orthodox, who see it as the natural result of too much philosophical speculation. Newman's non-scholastic theology carefully guarded against this tendency. In the *Arians* he says that the doctrines of the faith are 'facts, not opinions',[11] for God 'has made history to be doctrine'.[12] And so 'Christianity is eminently an objective religion. For the most part it tells us of persons and facts in simple words.'[13]

It was the heretical Arians who introduced philosophical terminology into theology, whereas their orthodox opponents Athanasius and Basil were unfamiliar with the terms. The epigraph Newman placed on the title-page of the *Grammar of*

---

[8] *Diff.* ii. 24.
[9] *TT* 137–299.
[10] *LD* xxvi. 276.
[11] *Ari.* 134.
[12] *PS* ii. 227.
[13] *Diff.* ii. 86.

Assent was the saying of St. Ambrose, himself a disciple of the Eastern Fathers, that 'It is not by logic that God has decided to save his people'. In his sermon on 'The Theory of Developments in Religious Doctrine' Newman warns against doctrinal propositions being confused with the idea of Christianity, 'which all such propositions taken together can but reach, and cannot exceed'. As we have already seen, without in any way rejecting dogma he is anxious to stress that

> the dogmatic statements of the Divine Nature used in our confessions, however multiplied, cannot say more than is implied in the original idea, considered in its completeness, without the risk of heresy. Creeds and dogmas live in the one idea which they are designed to express, and which alone is substantive; and are necessary only because the human mind cannot reflect upon that idea, except piecemeal, cannot use it in its oneness and entireness, nor without resolving it into a series of aspects and relations. And in matter of fact those expressions are never equivalent to it . . . and thus the Catholic dogmas are, after all, but symbols of a Divine fact, which, far from being compassed by those very propositions, would not be exhausted, nor fathomed, by a thousand.[14]

Indeed, Newman claims that a wariness with regard to doctrinal language does not necessarily argue an antipathy to dogma itself:

> . . . a reluctance to fix the phraseology of doctrine cannot be logically taken to imply an indisposition towards dogma itself; and in matter of fact it is historically contemporaneous with the most unequivocal dogmatic statements . . . The Epistles of Ignatius, for instance, who belongs to the Apostolical age of the Church, are in places unmistakeably dogmatic, without any use of technical terms . . . Indeed no better illustration can be given of that intrinsic independence of a fixed terminology which belongs to the Catholic Creed, than the writings of Athanasius himself . . . This great author scarcely uses any of the scientific phrases which have since been received in the Church and have become dogmatic . . .[15]

[14] *US* 331–2.
[15] *TT* 339.

In the *Grammar of Assent* he points out that the Church's liturgy is certainly dogmatic, yet without using the technical language of theology: without 'the subtlety, the aridity, the coldness of mere scholastic science', we find there 'the power of dogma' but it is 'addressed' to the 'imagination' not 'the pure intellect' and is intended to 'excite our devotion' not to 'interest our logical faculty'. Even the Church's creeds avoid the scientific and technical: the one exception that proves the rule was the introduction of the word 'consubstantial' into the Nicene Creed – 'the one instance of a scientific word having been introduced into the Creed from that day to this'.[16]

What Newman found on the contrary in the Eastern Fathers was the sense of Christianity as above all a mystery. It was the lack of this feeling that was characteristic of a heresy like that of the Arians:

> They did not admit into their theology the notion of mystery . . . It was useless to urge on them that they were reasoning about matters upon which they had no experimental knowledge; that we had no means of determining whether or how a spiritual being, really trine, could be numerically one, and therefore can only reason by means of our conceptions, and as if nothing were a fact which was inconceivable. It is a matter of faith that Father and Son are one, and reason does not therefore contradict it, because experience does not show us how to conceive of it. To us, poor creatures of a day, – who are but just now born out of nothing, and have everything to learn even as regards human knowledge, that such truths are incomprehensible to us, is no wonder.[17]

In the *Arians* Newman connected the loss of the sense of mystery that so marked the early Church with modern unbelief:

> If the early Church regarded the very knowledge of the truth as a fearful privilege, much more did it regard that truth itself as glorious and awful; and scarcely conversing about it to her children, shrank from the impiety of subjecting it to the hard gaze of the multitude . . . Now, we allow ourselves publicly to canvass the most solemn truths in a careless or fiercely argumentative way; truths, which it is as useless as it is unseemly to discuss in public.[18]

[16] *GA* 94, 97.
[17] *Ath.* ii. 44.
[18] *Ari.* 136.

The reason why it is so fruitless to subject the truths of revelation to this kind of rationalism is because it ignores the very nature of the Christian revelation:

> ... mystery is the necessary note of divine revelation, that is, mystery subjectively to the human mind: because, when the mind goes on freely to reason from language which only partially corresponds to eternal truths, and which cannot be adequately expressed in human words, it draws from one revealed information what is inconsistent with what it draws from another ...[19]

A due sense of mystery is ever for Newman the essential feature of true Christian spirituality: 'There is nothing ... which will make a greater difference in the temper, character, and habits of an individual, than the circumstance of his holding or not holding the Gospel to be mysterious.'[20]

Instead of encouraging too much speculation in theology, the East has always emphasised the overriding importance of tradition. Speaking of Athanasius, Newman points out that

> The fundamental idea with which he starts in the [Arian] controversy is a deep sense of the authority of Tradition, which he considers to have a definitive jurisdiction even in the interpretation of Scripture ... According to him, opposition to the witness of the Church, separation from its communion, private judgment overbearing the authorised catechetical teaching, the fact of a denomination, as men now speak, this is a self-condemnation ... It is not his aim ordinarily to *prove* doctrine by Scripture, nor does he appeal to the private judgment of the individual Christian in order to determine what Scripture means; but he assumes that there is a tradition, substantive, independent, and authoritative, such as to supply for us the true sense of Scripture in doctrinal matters – a tradition carried on from generation to generation by the practice of catechising, and by the other ministrations of Holy Church ... Revealed truth, to be what it professes, must have an uninterrupted descent from the Apostles ... for what is over and above nature must come from divine revelation; and, if so, it must descend from the very date when it was revealed, else it is but matter of opinion ...[21]

---

[19] *Ath.* ii. 92–3.
[20] *PS* iv. 292.
[21] *Ath.* ii. 51, 250, 150.

Modern Eastern theologians have been particularly critical of the way in which in the West the doctrine of the atonement has been subjected to analytical discussion. Writing again as an Anglican, Newman could not agree more:

> One might have thought that here at least somewhat of awful Mystery would have been allowed to hang over it; here at least some 'depth' of God's counsels would have been acknowledged and accepted on *faith*. For though the death of Christ manifests God's *hatred of sin*, as well as His love for man, (inasmuch as it was sin that made His death necessary, and the greater the sacrifice the greater must have been the evil that caused it,) yet *how* His death expiated our sins, and what satisfaction it was to God's *justice*, are surely subjects quite above us ... it is an event ever *mysterious* on account of its necessity . . .[22]

But if the East thinks that the West has shown too much interest in the how and why of the atonement, it is also surprised by the comparative lack of attention paid – at least until quite recently – to the resurrection. Before Vatican II Good Friday seemed almost to have a more central place in the worship of Western Catholicism than Easter itself. But Newman had discovered for himself in the Fathers, not to mention the New Testament, that 'those who omit the Resurrection in their view of the divine economy, are as really defective in faith as if they omitted the Crucifixion. On the Cross He paid the debt of the world, but as He could not have been crucified without first taking flesh, so again He could not ... apply His Atonement without first rising again.'[23] This was very different from the teaching of Evangelicals who 'think individuals are justified immediately by the great Atonement – justified by Christ's death and not, as St. Paul says, by means of His Resurrection'.[24] In fact, the Apostles preached the resurrection 'as if it were the main doctrine of the Gospel', and this was because the resurrection is 'the means by which the Atonement is applied to each of us'.[25] For 'Christ's bodily presence, which was limited to place', had to be 'exchanged for the manifold spiritual indwelling of the

[22] *Ess.* i. 66.
[23] *Ess.* i. 247.
[24] *Jfc.* 174.
[25] *Jfc.* 222.

Comforter within us',[26] that is to say the Holy Spirit. The Son returned to the Father at the resurrection, and at pentecost in his place came 'the Eternal Love whereby the Father and the Son have dwelt in each other',[27] in other words the Holy Spirit, whose 'coming is so really His coming, that we might as well say that He was not here in the days of His flesh, when He was visibly in this world, as deny that He is here now, when He is here by His Divine Spirit'.[28]

Newman's theology of the place of the Holy Spirit in Christ's redemption reflects the great tradition of the East. Christ, he preached,

> was born of the Spirit, and we too are born of the Spirit. He was justified by the Spirit, and so are we. He was pronounced the well-beloved Son, when the Holy Ghost descended on Him; and we too cry Abba, Father, through the Spirit sent into our hearts. He was led into the wilderness by the Spirit; He did great works by the Spirit; He offered Himself to death by the Eternal Spirit; He was raised from the dead by the Spirit; He was declared to be the Son of God by the Spirit of holiness on His resurrection: we too are led by the same Spirit into and through this world's temptations; we, too do our works of obedience by the Spirit; we die from sin, we rise again unto righteousness through the Spirit; and we are declared to be God's sons, – declared, pronounced, dealt with as righteous, – through our resurrection unto holiness in the Spirit . . . Christ Himself vouchsafes to repeat in each of us in figure and mystery all that He did and suffered in the flesh. He is formed in us, born in us, suffers in us, rises again in us, lives in us; and this not by a succession of events, but all at once: for He comes to us as a Spirit, all dying, all rising again, all living.[29]

The East (as we shall see) has always been much more careful about differentiating the three persons of the Trinity, and so Newman insists that the Spirit must not be seen as a replacement or substitute for the Son:

> Let us not for a moment suppose that God the Holy Ghost comes in such sense that God the Son remains away. No; He has

[26] *PS* ii. 222.
[27] *PS* ii. 229.
[28] *PS* iv. 248–9.
[29] *PS* v. 138–9.

not so come that Christ does not come, but rather He comes that Christ may come in His coming. Through the Holy Ghost we have communion with Father and Son ... The Holy Spirit causes, faith welcomes, the indwelling of Christ in the heart. Thus the Spirit does not take the place of Christ in the soul, but secures that place to Christ.[30]

While Western Christianity, both Catholic and Protestant, has so heavily concentrated on the crucifixion and the atonement, the East has been as concerned with the incarnation as the resurrection. Indeed, the two are very closely connected, as Newman shows: for while through the incarnation human nature was 'renewed' in Christ, 'glorious and wonderful beyond our thoughts', so as a result of the resurrection this same nature was raised up in glory, so that 'Henceforth, we dare aspire to enter into the heaven of heavens, and to live for ever in God's presence, because the first-fruits of our race is already there in the Person of His Only-begotten Son.'[31] In a sermon for Easter Sunday Newman explains that the resurrection is implied by and involved in the incarnation: 'Corruption had no power over that Sacred Body, the fruit of a miraculous conception.' In the resurrection the humanity of Christ was not discarded but was transfigured: 'the Divine Essence streamed forth (so to say) on every side, and environed His Manhood, as in a cloud of glory. So transfigured was His Sacred Body, that He who had deigned to be born of a woman, and to hang upon the cross, had subtle virtue in Him, like a spirit, to pass through the closed doors to His assembled followers.'[32]

In his classic study *The Mystical Theology of the Eastern Church* (1944; Eng. tr. 1957) Vladimir Lossky writes that the Orthodox Church 'never considers the humanity of Christ in abstraction, apart from His Godhead, whose fullness dwells in Him bodily'. Thus the stigmata, the outward bodily signs of the suffering Christ, have never characterised Eastern like some Western saints, for 'The cult of the humanity of Christ, is foreign to Eastern tradition; or rather, this deified humanity always assumes for the Orthodox Christian that some glorious form

[30] *PS* vi. 126.
[31] *PS* i. 176.
[32] *PS* ii. 142–3.

under which it appeared to the disciples on Mount Tabor: the humanity of the Son, manifesting forth that deity which is common to the Father and the Spirit'.[33] Newman knew only too well from his experience of liberal Anglicanism how a one-sided concentration on the humanity of Christ could so easily lead to the depreciation of his divinity:

> we have well-nigh forgotten the sacred truth, graciously disclosed for our support, that Christ is the Son of God in His Divine Nature, as well as His human . . . We speak of Him in a vague way as God, which is true, but not the whole truth; and, in consequence, when we proceed to consider His humiliation, we are unable to carry on the notion of His personality from heaven to earth. He who was but now spoken of as God, without mention of the Father from whom He is, is next described as if a creature; but how do these distinct notions of Him hold together in our minds? . . . when we merely speak first of God, then of man, we seem to change the Nature without preserving the Person. In truth, His Divine Sonship is that portion of the sacred doctrine on which the mind is providentially intended to rest throughout, and so to preserve for itself His identity unbroken.[34]

The reference here to the omission of any 'mention of the Father from whom He is' and the insistence on 'His Divine Sonship' as the key to understanding the identity of Christ show particularly the influence of the Eastern Fathers. Western theology has traditionally commenced with the one divine nature, and moved on secondarily to the distinctions of persons in the Godhead. The East has always begun with the personal God who is the Father. The Father therefore has a son who possesses consequently the same divine nature. The Father also has a Spirit who proceeds from the Father as Father, and so from the Father through the Son, possessing consequently the same divine nature as Father and Son by virtue of the procession. Thus Eastern theology concentrates on the different persons, beginning with the Father and then going on to the other persons who all possess the same divine nature. Unlike in Western theology, this divine nature is consequential rather than primary and the unity of the nature is the result of the procession of the persons.

[33] Op.cit. (Cambridge and London: James Clarke, 1973), 149, 243.
[34] *PS* iii. 170.

In recent times a Catholic theologian like Karl Rahner has insisted on the importance of distinguishing the different functions of the three persons of the Trinity. In his own time Newman maintained the Eastern tradition. Pointing out that no problem was more acute for the early Christians than the apparent discrepancy between professing the oneness of God and belief in the Trinity, he wrote:

> Christianity began its teaching by denouncing polytheism as wicked and absurd; but the retort on the part of the polytheist was obvious: – Christianity taught a Divine Trinity: how was this consistent with its profession of a Monarchy? . . . Catholic theologians met this difficulty both before and after the Nicene Council, by insisting on the unity of origin, which they taught as existing in the Divine Triad, the Son and Spirit having a communicated divinity from the Father, and a personal unity with Him . . . It was for the same reason that the Father was called God absolutely, while the Second and Third Persons were designated by Their personal names of 'the Son', or 'the Word', and 'the Holy Ghost'; viz. because they are to be regarded, not as separated from, but as inherent in the Father.

Rather than the divine nature taking precedence over the persons of the Trinity, the divine nature was seen by the Greek Fathers as existing first of all in God the Father: 'instead of saying "Father, Son and Spirit, are one substance (unum)", they would say "In one God and Father are the Son and Spirit"; the words "One Father" standing not only for the Person of the Father, but connecting that sole Divine substance which is one with His Person'.[35]

This doctrine of the primacy of the Father was played down in the West because of its abuse by the Arians who questioned the divinity of Christ. But Newman was clear that 'what St. Irenaeus, St. Athanasius, and St. Basil taught, can never be put aside. It is as true now as when those great Fathers enunciated it; and if true, it cannot be ignored without some detriment to the fullness and symmetry of the Catholic dogma.' It is, he thought, of particular importance in understanding the incarnation:

> One obvious use of it is to facilitate to the imagination the descent of the Divine Nature to the human, as revealed in the

[35] *TT* 167–8, 170–1.

doctrine of the Incarnation; the Eternal Son of God becoming by a second birth the Son of God in time, is a line of thought which preserves to us the continuity of idea in the Divine Revelation; whereas, if we say abruptly that the Supreme Being became the Son of Mary, this, however true when taken by itself, still by reason of the infinite distance between God and man, acts in the direction of the Nestorian error of a Christ with two Persons, as certainly as the doctrine of the *Principatus*, when taken by itself, favours the Arian error of a merely human Christ.[36]

In the more popular language of the preacher he explained:

our Lord's Sonship is not only the guarantee to us of His Godhead, but also the condition of His incarnation. As the Son was God, so on the other hand was the Son suitably made man; it belonged to Him to have the Father's perfections, it became Him to assume a servant's form. We must beware of supposing that the Persons of the Ever-blessed and All-holy Trinity differ from each other only in this, that the Father is not the Son, and the Son is not the Father. They differ in this besides, that the Father *is* the Father, and the Son *is* the Son. While They are one in substance, Each has distinct characteristics which the Other has not. Surely those sacred Names have a meaning in them, and must not lightly be passed over.[37]

In the East, justifying grace has always been seen in terms of the deification or divinisation of the Christian by virtue of the indwelling of the Holy Spirit, and through the Spirit of the Father and the Son as well. This personal union with the Trinity is very different from the Western idea of grace as negatively a remedy for sin and as a mere quality of the soul. Newman, of course, had found the doctrine of the indwelling of the Spirit in the New Testament as well as in the Fathers: 'He pervades us . . . as light pervades a building, or as a sweet perfume the folds of some honourable robe; so that, in Scripture language, we are said to be in Him, and He in us.' The presence of the Holy Spirit necessarily involves the presence of the other two Persons of the Trinity, and Newman is emphatic that invisible as this 'indwelling' is, there is nothing unreal about it – 'we are assured of some real though mystical fellowship with the Father, Son,

---

[36] *TT* 178–9.
[37] *PS* vi. 58.

and Holy Spirit . . . so that . . . by a real presence in the soul . . .
God is one with every believer, as in a consecrated Temple.'[38]

In *Lectures on the Doctrine of Justification* Newman solves the
problem of justification, which of course was at the heart of the
Reformation, by invoking the great scriptural and patristic
doctrine of the divine indwelling, so long forgotten and
neglected in the West by both Protestants and Roman Catholics.
It had, after all, been

> the great promise of the Gospel, that the Lord of all, who had
> hitherto manifested Himself externally to His servants, should
> take up His abode in their hearts . . . Though He had come in
> our flesh, so as to be seen and handled, even this was not enough.
> Still He was external and separate; but after His ascension He
> descended again by and in His Spirit, and then at length the
> promise was fulfilled.[39]

Our redemption was then complete: the 'dreadful reality' of
original sin was overtaken by a 'new righteousness', a 'real
righteousness' which 'comes from the Holy and Divine Spirit', so
that our 'works, done in the Spirit of Christ, have a justifying
principle in them, and that is the presence of the All-holy Spirit',
which 'hallows those acts, that life, that obedience of which it is
the original cause, and which it orders and fashions'.[40] Thus the
rival Catholic and Protestant theologies of works and faith, both
deeply imbedded in a late medieval theology of grace, can be
circumvented by the rediscovery of the central New Testament
doctrine of the indwelling of the Holy Spirit, a doctrine that was
second-nature to the Eastern Fathers who knew nothing of the
modern problem of justification: 'the presence of the Holy Ghost
shed abroad in our hearts, the Author both of faith and of
renewal, this is really that which makes us righteous, and . . . our
righteousness is the possession of that presence.' Justification,
then, 'is wrought by the power of the Spirit, or rather by His
presence within us', while 'faith and renewal are both present also,
but as fruits of it'.[41] The 'connection' between 'justification and
renewal' is that they are 'both included in that one great gift of

[38] *PS* ii. 222, 35.
[39] *PS* iv. 168.
[40] *PS* v. 156–8.
[41] *Jfc.* 137–8.

God, the indwelling of Christ' through the Holy Spirit 'in the Christian soul', which constitutes 'our justification and sanctification, as its necessary results'.[42]

If the answer to the contentious problem of justification is that justification consists in the divine indwelling, this justification in fact comes through the sacraments. Human flesh was divinised by the incarnation, and our own personal divinisation is achieved sacramentally:

> Our Lord, by becoming man, has found a way whereby to sanctify that nature, of which His own manhood is the pattern specimen. He inhabits us personally, and His inhabitation is effected by the channel of the Sacraments.

Through 'this indwelling', Christ is the 'immediate' source of 'spiritual life to each of His elect individually'. Thus, 'while we are in the flesh, soul and body become, by the indwelling of the Word, so elevated above their natural state, so sacred, that to profane them is a sacrilege'.[43]

Newman's own deeply sacramental theology was formed to a considerable extent by the writings of the Alexandrian Fathers, where he learned of 'the mystical or sacramental principle', according to which 'Holy Church in her sacraments . . . will remain, even to the end of the world, after all but a symbol of those heavenly facts which fill eternity'.[44] This profoundly sacramental vision meant that Newman never saw the sacraments of the Church apart from the larger sacramental reality, and particularly from the primordial sacrament, the Church herself. As for baptism, Newman saw it as the primary sacrament because through it the Christian receives the gift of the Holy Spirit. In a sermon on the words in St. Paul's first letter to the Corinthians, 'By one Spirit are we all baptised into one body', Newman expresses it like this:

> As there is One Holy Ghost, so there is one only visible Body of Christians . . . and one Baptism which admits men into it. This is implied in the text . . . But more than this is taught us in it; not only that the Holy Ghost is in the Church, and that Baptism admits into it, but that the Holy Ghost admits by

[42] *Jfc.* 154.
[43] *Ath.* ii. 193, 195
[44] *Apo.* 36–7.

means of Baptism, that the Holy Ghost baptises; in other words,
that each individual member receives the gift of the Holy Ghost
as a preliminary step, a condition, or means of his being
incorporated into the Church; or, in our Saviour's words, that no
one can enter, except to be regenerated in order to enter it.[45]

Modern Western Catholic theologians now follow the Eastern
tradition in grouping together as the three sacraments of
initiation, baptism, confirmation, and eucharist. Newman took
the same line as an Anglican:

> Confirmation seals in their fulness, winds up and consigns,
> completes the entire round of those sanctifying gifts which are
> begun, which are given inchoately in Baptism . . . it is properly
> an integral part of the Baptismal rite; I do not say of the essence,
> or an essential part, of Baptism, but an integral part, just as a
> hand is an integral part of our body, yet may be amputated
> without loss of life. And in ancient times it was administered at
> the time of Baptism, as its ratification.

He regrets that in the Church of England it is not
administered at an early age as in the Roman Catholic Church,
'but we, having no rite of penance, seem to substitute this'. As to
the particular grace given in confirmation, it 'is directed to arm
the Christian against his . . . enemies, which, when entering into
his field of trial, he at once meets'.[46] Newman hardly refers to
confirmation in his Anglican writings, but he does urge an early
age for reception of the sacrament, with the implication that it is
after all only the confirming of baptism: 'When persons are
young, before their minds are formed, ere they have sullied their
baptismal robe, and contracted bad habits, this is the time for
Confirmation, which conveys to them grace whereby they may
perform that "good work" which Baptism has begun in them.'[47]
Newman here is much closer to the Eastern tradition that
confirmation should closely follow baptism than to the
contemporary Western Catholic idea that it is a sacrament which
confirms a commitment taken at a mature age. The difference is
symptomatic of the divergence between the mystery-orientated
East and the rationalising West.

---

[45] *PS* iii. 271.
[46] *LD* vi. 80.
[47] *PS* iv. 63.

Newman's conception of the Church as primarily the communion of those who have received the Spirit in baptism is again the view of the East and was very different from the heavily institutional and juridical ecclesiology that had dominated Western Catholic thinking since Trent. As an Anglican, Newman preached that the Church 'is a visible body, invested with, or ... existing in invisible privileges', for 'the Church would cease to be the Church, did the Holy Spirit leave it', since 'its outward rites and forms are nourished and animated by the living power which dwells within it'.[48] Indeed, the Church is the Holy Spirit's 'especial dwelling-place'.[49] For while Christ came 'to die for us; the Spirit came to make us one in Him who had died and was alive, that is, to form the Church'. The Church, then, is 'the one mystical body of Christ ... quickened by the Spirit' – and it is 'one' by virtue of the Holy Spirit 'giving it *life*'.[50]

But although Newman had an Eastern pneumatic theology of the Church, he was also very well aware of the less mystical, less spiritual aspects of the Church militant. Again, writing as an Anglican, he was anxious to stress as well that the Church 'is a visible body, and, to appearance, an institution of this world'.[51] It is a 'Kingdom which Christ has set up' – or rather, 'a new kingdom has been established, not merely different from all kingdoms before it, but contrary to them; a paradox in the eyes of man, – the visible rule of the invisible Saviour'.[52] Instead of the gospel being simply 'left to the world at large', once it had been 'recorded ... in the Bible' –

> Christ formed a body; He secured that body from dissolution by the bond of a Sacrament. He committed the privileges of His spiritual Kingdom and the maintenance of His faith as a legacy to this baptised society ... Christianity has not been spread, as other systems, in an isolated manner, or by books; but from a centre, by regularly formed bodies, descendants of the three thousand, who, after St. Peter's preaching on the day of

[48] *PS* iii. 224; v. 41.
[49] *PS* iii. 270.
[50] *PS* iv. 170, 174, 171.
[51] *PS* ii. 391.
[52] *PS* vi. 313–4.

Pentecost, joined themselves to the Apostles' doctrine and fellowship.[53]

And so, although Newman's concept of the inner nature of the Church belongs more to the mystical theology of the Eastern Church than to the juridical ecclesiology of the Latin Church, he is by no means without a very keen awareness of the external institutional reality of the Church. For, humanly speaking, the Church 'is a visible body, and, to appearance, an institution of this world'.[54] Since, therefore, Christ 'has set up a kingdom in the world', 'a counter kingdom' to the 'kingdoms of this world',[55] this kingdom is far from being solely a spiritual one, even while ultimately it depends on the Spirit for its existence. Indeed, Newman declares, 'It is as unmeaning to speak of an invisible kingdom on earth, as of invisible chariots and horsemen, invisible swords and spears, invisible palaces; to be a kingdom at all it must be visible, if the word has any true meaning.' Certainly Scripture speaks of 'the visible appearance and display of . . . one kingdom in all lands'. In spite of his deeply sacramental theology of the mystical nature of the Church, Newman is unequivocal about the hierarchical and institutional character of the Church as well:

> If we will be scriptural in our view of the Church, we must consider that it is a kingdom, that its officers have great powers and high gifts, that they are charged with the custody of Divine Truth, that they are all united together, and that the nations are subject to them. If we reject this kind of ministry, as inapplicable to the present day, we shall in vain go to Scripture to find another.

The Gospels clearly indicate 'the imperial nature of Christ's kingdom', and Newman asks: 'Has there not, in fact, been a great corporation, or continuous body politic, all over the world, from the Apostles' days to our own, bearing the name of Church – one, and one only?' And it is this Church which has obtained that 'universal dominion, or Catholicity' which 'all empires of this world have sought after'.[56]

[53] *PS* vii. 236–7.
[54] *PS* ii. 391.
[55] *PS* vii. 230; *SD* 229.
[56] *SD* 220, 224, 227–8, 235, 248.

Newman's idea of the Church, then, was of something more than a Spirit-filled communion. And this is the moment to answer the question: Why, if Newman was so deeply and profoundly influenced by the East, did he not become an Eastern Orthodox rather than a Roman Catholic?

First, the thought surely never even occurred to Newman. Writing four years after his reception into the Catholic Church to an Anglican correspondent thinking of also converting, he says bluntly: 'I will not go through the question of the Greek Church, because unless your conversion depended on it, I could not bring myself to contemplate the absurdity (as it seems to me) of an Anglican becoming a Greek.' He does not, however, deny that, given the unCatholic nature of the Church of England, 'a so-called Anglo catholic should leave his communion either for Greece or Rome'.[57] In fact, in view of the very strong Eastern sense of the different patriarchates and rites, Newman's response was by no means so anti-Orthodox as it might seem, since it is not unheard of for Orthodox, with perfect consistency, to advise Anglicans to seek reunion with their own Western patriarch, namely the Bishop of Rome. When Newman says 'Greek' we should say 'Orthodox' today, but the use of the ethnic word brings out the essential ethnicity of Orthodoxy, divided into autonomous ethnic or national churches. Thus an Anglican who wishes to convert to Orthodoxy has to decide which Orthodox church to join – the Greek or Russian or which? Although, of course, Orthodoxy has spread through the diaspora into the West, especially North America, it still looks very unconvincing as a catholic or universal Church, bound up as it is in particular cultural and national traditions – what Newman calls the 'consecration of the principle of nationalism'.[58] It was not even clear to Newman if Orthodox would regard their church as the Catholic Church, as it seemed they had given up the idea of 'the Catholicity of the Church', on the ground that although there had once been 'One Catholic Church' in the world, it had 'died, and the Russo-Greek Church is all that remains of it'.[59] These words were

[57] *LD* xiii. 296.
[58] *HS* i. 203.
[59] *LD* xxx. 109, 112 .

written with reference to Newman's editing and publishing in 1882 his fellow convert friend William Palmer's *Notes of a Visit to the Russian Church in the Years 1840, 1841.*

Second, if the Orthodox Church lacks the role of catholicity, it also lacks what Newman called 'political life, such as an ecclesiastic body ought to have'.[60] In his great ecclesological essay, the 1877 preface to his *Via Media,* Newman attributed a 'triple office' to the Church – 'teaching, rule, and sacred ministry'. Christianity, then, 'is at once a philosophy, a political power, and a religious rite: as a religion, it is Holy; as a philosophy, it is Apostolic; as a political power, it is imperial, that is, One and Catholic'. The political office is vital if the Church is to preserve her independence and freedom of action, as is shown by the Orthodox Church, 'which has lost its political life, while its doctrine, and its ritual and devotional system, have little that can be excepted against'. But for Newman the Church, like 'a sovereign State' has 'to consolidate her several positions, to enlarge her territory, to keep up and to increase her various populations in this ever-dying, ever-nascent world, in which to be stationary is to lose ground, and to repose is to fail'. How such considerations reflect on Orthodoxy are only too obvious: apart from emigration, its sphere of influence has decreased rather than increased over the centuries, there has been practically no missionary activity in modern times, and its traditional Byzantine subservience to the state has left it defenceless and even discredited as an institution in the face of over a half a century of Communist persecution. But the unfavourable comparison made some years ago by the Russian novelist Alexander Solzhenitsyn between the Russian Orthodox and the Polish Catholic churches in their response to Communist persecution is hardly fair. For apart from other differences, the Polish church had an external centre of authority to look to for support. Thus Newman claims in the *Via Media* preface that Christianity's 'special centre of action' as a political power is the papacy.[61] If this is the case, then it is hardly surprising that the Orthodox Church is hopelessly ethnic and

---

[60] *LD* xxv. 5.
[61] *VM* i. xl, lxxx–lxxxi.

nationalistic in its lack of a strong centre of authority, with the ecumenical patriarchate of Constantinople enjoying prestige and respect but little or no effective power.

Third, there is the lack of a teaching authority in Orthodoxy. The Orthodox make much of episcopal collegiality and of councils, but in fact they have never been able since the great schism to hold a general or ecumenical council. It is indeed hard to see how they could do so without the presence of the Western Patriarch, whom, as Bishop of Rome, they recognise as 'primus inter pares', first among equals. Newman refers to this obvious lack of teaching in his *Essay on the Development of Christian Doctrine* when he points out that after the schism between East and West the Orthodox did not 'present more than a negative opposition' to Rome. The Orthodox churches have preserved orthodox doctrine in their liturgy and tradition, but in the absence of both pope and council a living teaching authority is no longer operative, which partly explains why Newman can say, 'Doctrine without its correspondent principle remains barren, if not lifeless, of which the Greek Church seems an instance.'[62]

Fourth, the word 'lifeless' in this quotation reminds one that Newman thought that *life* was an important note of the Church. Indeed, when he was already beginning to have doubts about Anglicanism, he once said that the 'burst of hidden life' revealed by the Oxford Movement in the Church of England was 'the greatest note of the Catholicity of our Church'.[63] As a Catholic, he argued that corruption was inseparable from a living Church: 'Things that do not admit of abuse have very little life in them.'[64] And it is this very quality of 'life' which he insists on as a pre-eminent note of the Church: 'The Church is emphatically a living body . . . she alone revives even if she declines; heretical and schismatical bodies cannot keep life.'[65] Judged by that criterion, too, Newman found Orthodoxy lacking: 'the Greeks show no signs of life, but remain shut up as if in the sepulchre of the past.'[66]

---

[62] *Dev.* 95, 181.
[63] For this quotation, see *Ker* 230.
[64] *Diff.* ii. 89.
[65] *Ess.* ii. 53–4.
[66] *LD* xxiv. 355.

6

Catholic Christianity

In a centenary profile of Newman, Owen Chadwick has recently maintained that Newman was looking for 'an ideal' church and that, although the Roman Catholic Church fell short of his ideal in practice, nevertheless he continued to believe that it was of all the Christian churches the closest to the ideal.[1] Do the facts support this assertion?

Newman's first real *doubt*, as opposed to difficulty, about the claim of the Church of England to be a real branch of the Catholic Church came in 1839 when, after an interval of four years, he returned to the study of the theological controversies of the fifth century, partly because he was hoping to rewrite *The Arians of the Fourth Century.* He was not thinking of the Church of Rome, about which he had written nothing controversial or polemical for the past four years. But during the course of his reading, 'for the first time a doubt came upon me of the tenableness of Anglicanism'. The usual objections to the Anglo-Catholic position concerned the events of the 16th century Reformation and how far the Elizabethan settlement had damaged the Catholic nature of the Anglican formularies and liturgy. The strength of the Anglo-Catholic case, on the other hand, appeared to rest on the historical character of the early Church, so different it seemed from the Tridentine Roman Church. As Newman was to recall in the *Apologia:*

> My stronghold was Antiquity; now here, in the middle of the fifth century, I found, as it seemed to me, Christendom of the sixteenth and the nineteenth centuries reflected. I saw my face in

[1] Owen Chadwick, Introduction to Susan Foister, *Cardinal Newman 1801–90: A Centenary Exhibition* (National Portrait Gallery Publications: London, 1990), 7.

that mirror, and I was a Monophysite. The Church of the *Via Media* was in the position of the Oriental communion, Rome was, where she now is; and the Protestants were the Eutychians.[2]

What disturbed Newman was the sight of Pope St. Leo upholding the Catholic faith, while the heretics divided into an extreme and a moderate party: was there conceivably an analogy here with modern Roman Catholicism and Protestantism at the two extremes and Anglicanism in the middle? It was certainly no more than a suggestive argument from analogy.

There was a worse shock to come: a review article in August 1839 by Nicholas Wiseman on the Donatist heresy in North Africa, but with particular reference to the Anglican position. At first Newman saw no special significance in it, as the Donatist schism from within the African church seemed to bear no resemblance to the conflict between Rome and the oriental Monophyites. But the friend who had lent him the review,

> pointed out the palmary words of St. Augustine, which were contained in one of the extracts made in the Review, and which had escaped my observation. "Securus judicat orbis terrarum." He repeated those words again and again, and, when he was gone, they kept ringing in my ears. "Securus judicat orbis terrarum"; they were words which went beyond the occasion of the Donatists: they applied to that of the Monophysites . . . They decided ecclesiastical questions on a simpler rule than that of Antiquity; nay, St. Augustine was one of the prime oracles of Antiquity; here then Antiquity was deciding against itself. What a light was hereby thrown upon every controversy in the Church! not that, for the moment, the multitude may not falter in their judgment, – not that, in the Arian hurricane, Sees more than can be numbered did not bend before its fury, and fall off from St. Athanasius, – not that the crowd of Oriental Bishops did not need to be sustained during the contest by the voice and the eye of St. Leo; but that the deliberate judgment, in which the whole Church at length rests and acquiesces, is an infallible prescription and a final sentence against such portions of it as protest and secede. Who can account for the impressions which are made on him? For a mere sentence, the words of St. Augustine, struck me with a power which I never had felt from any words before. To take a familiar instance, they were like the 'Turn again

[2] *Apo.* 108.

Whittington' of the chime; or, to take a more serious one, they were like the 'Tolle, lege, – Tolle, lege', of the child, which converted St. Augustine himself. "Securus judicat orbis terrarum!" By those great words of the ancient Father, interpreting and summing up the long and varied course of ecclesiastical history, the theory of the *Via Media* was absolutely pulverized.[3]

The words that made such a deep impression on Newman are not altogether easy to translate. Newman's own (free) rendering was: 'The universal Church is in its judgments secure of truth.'[4] The translation makes the point: it was the idea of *the Church*, not a part or branch of the Church, but the Church universal that struck Newman so powerfully.

It was not, of course, that Newman was unaware of the Roman Catholic argument from catholicity: it was just that the argument now struck him with a force that it never had before, since it now came from the very voice of that early apostolic Church to which Tractarianism appealed. As he explains in the *Apologia,* 'the Anglican disputant took his stand upon Antiquity or Apostolicity, the Roman upon Catholity'. Thus Anglicans argued that the Roman Catholic Church had added to the original apostolic doctrine, while Roman Catholics pointed out that the Anglican Church was manifestly uncatholic in its lack of universality. Newman's Tractarian position, then, was that the 'true Church, as defined in the Creeds, was both Catholic and Apostolic', but that 'England and Rome had divided these notes or prerogatives between them: the course lay thus, Apostolicity *versus* Catholicity'. It was not, naturally, that he

allowed the note of Catholicity really to belong to Rome, to the disparagement of the Anglican Church; but I considered that the special point or plea of Rome in the controversy was Catholicity, as the Anglican plea was Antiquity. Of course I contended that the Roman idea of Catholicity was not ancient and apostolic. It was in my judgment at the utmost only natural, becoming, expedient, that the whole of Christendom should be united in one visible body; while such a unity might, on the other hand, be nothing more than a mere heartless and political combination. For myself, I held with the Anglican divines, that,

[3] *Apo.* 110–11.
[4] *Ess.* ii. 101.

in the Primitive Church, there was a very real mutual independence between its separate parts, though, from a dictate of charity, there was in fact a close union between them . . . The unity of the Church lay, not in its being a polity, but in its being a family, a race, coming down by apostolical descent from its first founders and bishops.[5]

The central issue for Newman as a Tractarian was the nature of the Church, and never the papacy, although this presented no particular difficulties and he easily accepted papal authority and jurisdiction when he became a Catholic. For Roman Catholics the faith was inseparable from the Church, but for Anglicans the faith was 'the foundation of the Church as well as of the individual' and the individual was 'bound to obey the Church, only so far as the Church holds to the faith'. This was the so-called 'doctrine of Fundamentals', according to which 'the Truth [is] entirely objective and detached, not lying hid in the bosom of the Church as if one with her, clinging to her and (as it were) lost in her embrace, but as being sole and unapproachable as on the Cross or at the Resurrection, with the Church close by, but in the background'. These words were written in 1838 when Newman was aware of the 'difficulty . . . in determining what is the fundamental faith'.[6] What, however, if antiquity itself did not support this view of the relationship of faith and church?

Even after the two shocks of the summer of 1839, Newman could still write in 1840 that the Anglican 'strong point is the argument from the past, that of the Romanists is the argument from the present. It is a fact, however it is to be explained, that Rome has added to the Creed; and it is a fact, however it be justified, that we are estranged from the great body of Christians over the world.'[7] But his reading had shown him all too clearly 'the hitch in the Anglican argument':

> The difficulty in question had affected my view both of Antiquity and Catholicity; for, while the history of St. Leo showed me that the deliberate and eventual consent of the great body of the Church ratified a doctrinal decision as a part of revealed truth, it also showed that the rule of Antiquity was not

[5] *Apo.* 101–2.
[6] *Ess.* i. 209–10.
[7] *Ess.* ii. 6.

infringed, though a doctrine had not been publicly recognised as so revealed, till centuries after the time of the Apostles. Thus, whereas the Creeds tell us that the Church is One, Holy, Catholic, and Apostolic, I could not prove that the Anglican communion was an integral part of the One Church, on the ground of its teaching being Apostolic or Catholic, without reasoning in favour of what are commonly called the Roman corruptions; and I could not defend our separation from Rome and her faith without using arguments prejudicial to those great doctrines concerning our Lord, which are the very foundation of the Christian religion.[8]

In reaction against the Nestorian view that the divine and human natures of Christ are separate, the Monophysites held that after the incarnation Christ had only one nature, a divine nature in which the human nature was absorbed. Pope Leo the Great's formulation of the orthodox Christian doctrine that Christ is one person in two natures both divine and human was accepted by the Council of Chalcedon. Here was a crucial and essential part of basic Christian doctrine which had only been defined formally in the fifth century by the Church. In other words, here was an important development of doctrine guaranteed only by the Church but which was as much part of Anglicanism as of Roman Catholicism.

As is well known, Newman's own conversion to Rome was bound up in the development of his own thoughts on the key problem of development of doctrine. If Anglicanism could not be defended without invoking the idea of doctrinal development, was there anything in principle against the later developments of doctrine to be found in Roman Catholicism? In May 1843 he wrote privately to John Keble that he was 'far *more* sure that England is in schism, than that the Roman additions to the Primitive Creed may not be developments, arising out of a keen and vivid realising of the Divine Deposition of faith'.[9] In the preceding February he had already preached the last of his *Oxford University Sermons*, 'The Theory of Developments in Religious Doctrine'. It was the first time that he had turned his full attention to the subject. Hardly a mere question of academic

[8] *Apo.* 138–9.
[9] Cit. in *Ker* 274.

interest, it was now literally a matter of life or death as far as his continuing membership of the Church of England was concerned.

It was certainly, though, far from the first time that he had thought about the problem. In his first book, *The Arians,* he had at least recognised the phenomenon. A year later in 1834 he wrote that 'the greater part of the theological and ecclesiastical system, which is implicitly contained in the writings and acts of the Apostles ... was developed at various times according to circumstances'.[10] And in one of the *Tracts for the Times* of the same year, he says that the 'articles of faith' which 'are necessary to secure the Church's purity, according to the rise of successive heresies and error', were 'all hidden, as it were, in the Church's bosom from the first, and brought out into form according to the occasion'.[11] Again, in the *Apologia,* he points out that in an article published in 1836 he had clearly acknowledged the Roman Catholic answer to objections that the Church of Rome 'has departed from Primitive Christianity', namely, that such apparent departures may be seen as 'developments of gospel truth' which are also to be found in Anglicanism, since 'the Anglican system itself is not found complete in those early centuries'.[12]

After the crisis of doubt of 1839, the issue effectively narrowed down to the question of the development of doctrine: were specifically Roman Catholic doctrines illegitimate accretions and additions, or were they authentic developments from scriptural and apostolic doctrines? Why were those doctrines, which Anglicans shared with Roman Catholics, but which were sometimes less clearly to be found in Scripture and the Fathers, not also accretions and additions?

Newman's idea in his *Lectures on the Prophetical Office* (1837) of a 'Prophetical Tradition' existing within the Church had allowed in principle for developments taking place as a normal occurrence. But in his 1843 sermon he went even further, saying that developments were not simply explanations of doctrine already formulated but further doctrines implied by and arising

---

[10] *LD* iv. 180.
[11] *VM* ii. 40.
[12] *Apo.* 108.

out of those original dogmas. In this lengthy sermon, one of the most original and brilliant of his writings, Newman applies to the problem of doctrinal development a key epistemological distinction he had already made in one of the earlier *Oxford University Sermons* on the difference between 'Implicit and Explicit Reason'. The differentiation is crucial to his whole idea of the development of doctrine. Thus he maintains in 'The Theory of Developments in Religious Doctrine' that, 'naturally as the inward idea of divine truth . . . passes into explicit form by the activity of our reflective powers, still such an actual delineation is not essential to its genuineness and perfection', so that a 'peasant may have such a true impression, yet be unable to give any intelligible account of it'. Indeed, the 'impression made upon the mind need not even be recognised' by the person 'possessing it'. Such 'unperceived impressions' are commonplace in life: thus people may not even be 'conscious' of 'an idea' of which they are actually 'possessed'. Nor is the 'absence, or partial absence, or incompleteness of dogmatic statements' any 'proof of the absence of impressions or implicit judgments, in the mind of the Church. Even centuries might pass without the formal expression of a truth, which had been all along the secret life of millions of faithful souls.'[13]

By the end of 1844 Newman was practically certain that the Church of England, far from being a branch of the Catholic Church, was in fact in schism and that the Roman Catholic Church was the same church as the church of the Fathers. To test this conviction once and for all, he decided to write a study of the development of doctrine, which he published after his conversion in an unfinished state as *An Essay on the Development of Christian Doctrine* (1845). At the beginning Newman points out that the idea of doctrinal development is not a new idea which he is putting forward, since it has been implicitly assumed more or less by theologians through the ages. However, not only was Newman the first theologian to pay sustained attention to the problem, but his view of development is much more complex and subtle than both the logical explication theory of the Scholastics and Bossuet's principle of clarification. The latter

[13] *US* 320–1, 323.

coincided more or less with Newman's previous idea, which he had come to think was inadequate because it did not account for the sheer extent of doctrinal development: the former theory, which maintained that later dogmatic formulations are logically deduced from previous formulations, was obviously too rigid for the actual historical facts.

The basic historical fact with which Newman begins is the sheer extent apparently of change and variation in Christianity over the centuries.[14] The question then naturally arises whether there has been any 'real continuity of doctrine' since the time of the Apostles.[15] This has led to Protestants 'dispensing with historical Christianity altogether, and ... forming a Christianity from the Bible alone' – which is understandable given that 'the Christianity of history' is certainly 'not Protestantism'.[16] Anglicans, on the other hand, have traditionally appealed to the famous dictum of Vincent of Lerins that 'Christianity is what has been held always, everywhere, and by all', a rule which

> is irresistible against Protestantism, and in one sense indeed it is irresistible against Rome also, but in the same sense it is irresistible against England. It strikes at Rome through England. It admits of being interpreted in one of two ways: if it be narrowed for the purpose of disproving the catholicity of the Creed of Pope Pius, it becomes also an objection to the Athanasian; and if it be relaxed to admit the doctrines retained by the English Church, it no longer excludes certain doctrines of Rome which that Church denies. It cannot at once condemn St. Thomas and St. Bernard, and defend St. Athanasius and St. Gregory Nazianzen.[17]

If the fact of development is the basic fact, the fundamental idea lying behind the *Essay* is precisely Newman's concept of an idea such as that of Christianity. He argues that a living idea necessarily grows into 'a body of thought', which 'will after all be little more than the proper representative of one idea, being in substance what that idea meant from the first, its complete image as seen in a combination of diversified aspects, with the suggestions and corrections of many minds, and the illustration

---

[14] For the following discussion of development see *Ker* 302–6.
[15] *Dev.* 5.
[16] *Dev.* 7.
[17] *Dev.* 11–12.

of many experiences'. It is the 'process ... by which the aspects of an idea are brought into consistency and form' which Newman calls 'its development, being the germination and maturation of some truth or apparent truth on a large mental field'. But he warns, 'this process will not be a development, unless the assemblage of aspects, which constitute its ultimate shape, really belongs to the idea from which they start'. Far from being passive,

> A development will have this characteristic, that, its action being in the busy scene of human life, it cannot progress at all without cutting across, and thereby destroying or modifying and incorporating with itself existing modes of thinking and operating. The development then of an idea is not like an investigation worked out on paper, in which each successive advance is a pure evolution from a foregoing, but it is carried on through and by means of communities of men and their leaders and guides; and it employs their minds as its instruments, and depends upon them, while it uses them.

Characteristic of Newman's thought is the point that the development of an idea necessarily involves conflict: 'It is the warfare of ideas under their various aspects striving for the mastery, each of them enterprising, engrossing, imperious, more or less incompatible with the rest ...' The development is not carried out in a vacuum: 'an idea not only modifies, but is modified, or at least influenced, by the state of things in which it is carried out, and is dependent in various ways on the circumstances which surround it.' This means that there may be 'the risk of corruption from intercourse with the world around', but 'such a risk must be encountered if a great idea is duly to be understood, and much more if it is to be fully exhibited. It is elicited and expanded by trial, and battles into perfection and supremacy.' This brings Newman to the conclusion that an idea is actually brought out rather than obscured by development, as he argues in a famous passage which ends with a sentence that is often quoted, although quite misleadingly when the preceding sentence is omitted.

> It is indeed sometimes said that the stream is clearest near the spring. Whatever use may fairly be made of this image, it does not apply to the history of a philosophy or belief, which on the

contrary is more equable, and purer, and stronger, when its bed
has become deep, and broad, and full. It necessarily rises out of
an existing state of things, and for a time savours of the soil. Its
vital element needs disengaging from what is foreign and
temporary . . . It remains perhaps for a time quiescent; it tries, as
it were, its limbs, and proves the ground under it, and feels its
way. From time to time it makes essays which fail, and are in
consequence abandoned. It seems in suspense which to go; it
wavers, and at length strikes out in one definite direction. In
time it enters upon strange territory; points of controversy alter
their bearing; parties rise and fall around it; dangers and hopes
appear in new relations; and old principles reappear under new
forms. It changes with them in order to remain the same. In a
higher world it is otherwise, but here below to live is to change,
and to be perfect is to have changed often.[18]

Given Newman's view of development as integral to the life of
an idea, then there is what he calls an 'antecedent probability' in
favour of the development of doctrine. For, 'If Christianity is a
fact, and impresses an idea of itself on our minds and is a
subject-matter of exercises of the reason, that idea will in course
of time expand into a multitude of ideas, and aspects of ideas,
connected and harmonious with one another, and in themselves
determinate and immutable, as is the objective fact itself which
is thus represented.' The more an idea claims to be 'living, the
more various will be its aspects', for 'whole objects do not create
in the intellect whole ideas, but are . . . thrown . . . into a number
of statements, strengthening, interpreting, correcting each other,
and with more or less exactness approximating, as they
accumulate, to a perfect image'. It is not possible to 'teach except
by aspects or views, which are not identical with the thing itself
which we are teaching'. Since Christianity in particular is not a
local but a universal religion, 'it cannot but vary in its relations
and dealings towards the world around it, that is, it will
develop', for 'Principles require a very various application
according as persons and circumstances vary, and must be
thrown into new shapes according to the form of society which
they are to influence'. New problems and questions arise which
'must be answered, and, unless we suppose a new revelation,

[18] *Dev.* 38–40.

answered by means of the revelation which we have, that is, by development'. Thus Scripture does not solve the difficulties which are raised about its own authority and interpretation, but 'in matter of fact the decision has been left to time, to the slow process of thought, to the influence of mind upon mind, the issues of controversy, and the growth of opinion'. And the fact that 'Scripture needs completion' suggests that the 'defect or inchoateness in its doctrines' constitutes 'an antecedent probability in favour of a development of them'. In the Bible itself we find a 'prophetic Revelation' in the form of 'a process of development', in which

> the earlier prophecies are pregnant texts out of which the succeeding announcements grow; they are types. It is not that first one truth is told, then another; but the whole truth or large portions of it are told at once, yet only in rudiments, or in miniature, and they are expanded and finished in their parts, as the course of revelation proceeds.

Indeed, 'the whole Bible, not its prophetical portions only, is written on the principle of development. As the Revelation proceeds, it is ever new, yet ever old.' Moreover, the sayings of Christ and the Apostles

> are of a typical structure . . . predictions as well as injunctions of doctrine. If then the prophetic sentences have had that development which has really been given them, first by succeeding revelations, and then by the event, it is probable antecedently that those doctrinal, political, ritual, and ethical sentences, which have the same structure, should admit the same expansion.

It is not, then, surprising that after the ascension it is impossible 'to fix an historical point at which the growth of doctrine ceased, and the rule of faith was once for all settled', or to find 'one doctrine . . . which starts complete at first, and gains nothing afterwards from the investigations of faith and the attacks of heresy'.[19]

Having established that an 'idea' like that of Christianity must of its nature admit of developments, Newman now proceeds to argue that if Christianity claims to be an objectively true

[19] *Dev.* 55–6, 58, 60, 62, 64–6, 68.

revelation, then there must be some means of authenticating and ratifying developments. In other words, development implies authority. For if there is an antecedent probability of developments, then 'this is a strong antecedent argument in favour of a provision in the Dispensation for putting a seal of authority upon those developments'. After all, Christianity 'is a revelation which comes to us as a revelation, as a whole, objectively, and with a profession of infallibility', since, 'unlike other revelations ... except the Jewish, of which it is a continuation, [it] is an objective religion, or a revelation with credentials'.

> We are told that God has spoken. Where? In a Book? We have tried it and it disappoints; it disappoints us, that most holy and blessed gift, not from fault of its own, but because it is used for a purpose for which it was not given ... The Church undertakes that office; she does what none else can do, and this is the secret of her power.

Otherwise, 'a revelation is not given, if there be no authority to decide what it is that is given'. And so, in order to distinguish true from false developments, a 'supreme authority' is necessary: without an 'infallible chair' the only unity possible is 'a comprehension of opinions' such as the 'hollow uniformity' of the Church of England. Nor is 'the notion of development under infallible authority' an implausible 'hypothesis ... to account for the rise of Christianity and the formation of its theology'.[20]

History shows how the various developments that took place in the East and West are 'suggestive, or correlative, or confirmatory, or illustrative of each other'; whereas 'the heretical doctrines were confessedly barren and short-lived, and could not stand their ground against Catholicism'. Since the great schism between East and West, only the Roman Catholic Church has been able to continue and to validate doctrinal developments. In the middle ages the Orthodox Church seemed to 'present [no] more than a negative opposition' to Rome. 'And now in like manner the Tridentine Creed is met by no rival developments; there is no antagonist system.' Protests against Roman Catholicism there are in abundance but 'little of positive

[20] *Dev.* 79–80, 88–90, 92.

teaching anywhere' else. Newman concludes that there is undeniably a 'very strong presumption' that, 'if there must be and are in fact developments in Christianity, the doctrines propounded by successive Popes and Councils . . . are they'.[21]

Newman's fundamental reason, then, for converting to the Roman Catholic Church was the argument from development, and consequently the argument from authority. If an idea like that of Christianity is to be a living idea, it must evidence development. But developments have to be distinguished from corruptions, and although Newman did indeed offer seven 'Tests' or 'Notes' — which he clearly intended to be tentative rather than exhaustive criteria[22] — this did not remove the need for a living authority to pronounce on the legitimacy of the developments in question. Since no other church apart from the Roman Catholic Church claimed in practice to be able to do so, this seemed to Newman to present a prima facie case for the claim of the Church of Rome to be the uniquely authoritative Church of Christ.

All this seems very far from Owen Chadwick's assertion that Newman was looking for an 'ideal' Church. Indeed, in an important sense, the opposite seems to be the case. After all, what had troubled Newman as an Anglican was not only Rome's alleged additions to the creed but also her apparent corruption in practice. As part of his Evangelical conversion at the age of 15, he had imbibed the idea that the Pope was the Antichrist of the Scripture prophecies. This belief gradually weakened but lingered till 1843. As a Tractarian, he records in the *Apologia*, he 'thought the essence of her offence to consist in the honours which she paid to the Blessed Virgin and the Saints; and the more I grew in devotion, both to the Saints and to our Lady, the more impatient was I at the Roman practices, as if those glorified creations of God must be gravely shocked . . . at the undue veneration of which they were the objects'.[23] He knew, however, that ' a broad distinction had to be drawn between the actual state of belief and of usage in the countries which were in

[21] *Dev.* 93, 95–6.
[22] See Ian Ker, *The Achievement of John Henry Newman* (Notre Dame: University of Notre Dame Press, 1990; London: Collins, 1990), 113.
[23] *Apo.* 57–8.

communion with the Roman Church, and her formal dogmas; the latter did not cover the former'. For instance, although actual physical pain was not involved in the doctrine of purgatory as it had been defined by the Council of Trent, still pictures of souls in flames were very much part of popular Roman Catholicism. This was one example of 'the living system' which he called 'Roman corruption'.[24] If, then, it appeared as if the Church of England lacked the note of Catholicity, it also looked as if the Church of Rome possessed the 'Note of idolatry'.[25] When the theory of the 'Via Media' had to be abandoned, Newman fell back on his 'anti-Romanism', that 'practical principle' of 'pure Protestantism', which 'still had great hold' on him, even 'though it was only a negative ground'. However, even before the crisis of the summer of 1839, he had come to see that, 'from the nature of the case, the true Vicar of Christ must ever to the world seem like Antichrist, and be stigmatized as such, because a resemblance must ever exist between an original and a forgery; and thus the fact of such a calumny was almost one of the notes of the Church'.[26] But intellectual conviction was one thing, instinctive ingrained prejudice another. And it was not until 1844 that his difficulty over Roman Catholic veneration of Mary and the saints was finally overcome.

There was another practical objection to the Church of Rome and that was her political involvement. She seemed quite happy, for instance, to ally herself with irreligious anti-Anglican liberals and radicals in order to further 'Catholicism by violence and intrigue'.[27] The charge of this kind of unscrupulosity was, of course, traditionally levelled against Rome.

Even when all the objections to Rome had lost their force, Newman still felt no human attraction to the Church as he knew her: 'I have no existing sympathies with Roman Catholics. I hardly ever, even abroad, was at one of their services – I know none of them. I do not like what I hear of them.'[28] Allowing for some element of exaggeration in a private letter written in the

[24] *Apo.* 100–1.
[25] *Apo.* 107.
[26] *Apo.* 115.
[27] *Apo.* 117.
[28] Cit. in *Ker* 293.

anguish of impending separation from the Church of England, it was not attraction to the Roman Church but 'a stern necessity' that was taking him from 'all I love' to 'those whom I do not know and of whom I expect very little'.[29] Not only were his feelings very negative about the actual historical communion he was joining, but he had extraordinarily little idea positively of any spiritual benefits he would receive, as this letter about the reservation of the Blessed Sacrament shows:

> We went over not realising those privileges which we have found *by* going. I never allowed my mind to dwell on what I might gain of blessedness – but certainly, if I had thought much upon it, I could not have fancied the extreme, ineffable comfort of being in the same house with Him who cured the sick and taught His disciples . . . When I have been in Churches abroad, I have religiously abstained from acts of worship, though it was a most soothing comfort to go into them – nor did I know what was going on; I neither understood nor tried to understand the Mass service – and I did not know, or did not observe, the tabernacle Lamp – but now after tasting of the awful delight of worshipping God in His Temple, how unspeakably cold is the idea of a Temple without that Divine Presence![30]

It is, of course, very common for people to become Catholics because they are drawn to the liturgy and sacramentality of Catholicism, but this was hardly even a factor for Newman, whose practical experience of the life of the Catholic Church hardly led him to see her as an 'ideal' Church, spiritually or in any other way. Imaginatively, what drew Newman was his recognition of the identity of the Roman Catholic Church with the early Church. More theologically, it was his understanding that Christianity must develop doctrinally if there is any life in its idea, and that there must be an infallible authority to confirm the genuineness of the developments, unless the idea is to lose its essential identity.

Anyway Newman already saw himself as a 'Catholic' while he was a Tractarian Anglican. He had learned his Catholicism from the Fathers, although he was not fully aware of how the sacramentalism of the early Church was expressed in practice in

[29] Cit. in *Ker* 297.
[30] *LD* xi. 131.

the Roman Catholic Church of his time. His deconversion from Anglicanism certainly had a very concrete aspect – his disillusionment over the Jerusalem bishopric and the condemnation of Tract 90. But his actual conversion to Rome was definitely not based on any first-hand experience of Roman Catholicism – although it is true that his Mediterranean tour of 1832–3 had helped to dispel many of his prejudices.[31]

It was only after he became a Roman Catholic that Newman discovered other deficiencies in his new church. But his earlier impressions of exaggerated devotions were not dispelled. Instead, however, he came to work out a veritable theology of corruption, according to which the kind of corruptions which had once convinced him that the Roman Catholic Church was the Church of the Antichrist are now seen practically as notes of the true Church![32] For corruption is now viewed as inseparable from a living Church: 'Things that do not admit of abuse have very little life in them.'[33] And it is this very quality of life which Newman insists on as a special note of the Church: 'The Church is emphatically a living body ... she alone revives even if she declines; heretical and schismatical bodies cannot keep life.'[34] As an Anglican, Newman had been very concerned to show that the Church of England had 'life' and 'a living principle', a note of the Church 'equal to any'.[35]

Not only did Christ predict scandals, but in the parable of the tares and the wheat, for example, he spoke of the Church 'as in its very constitution made up of good and bad'. The corruption of the Church had in fact existed from the time of Judas Iscariot and was so 'bound up with the very idea of Christianity' as to be 'almost a dogma'.[36] Given that the world is sinful, once 'it has poured into the Church, it has insulted and blasphemed the religion which it professed, in a special way, in which heathenism cannot insult it'. One would expect to find greater corruption in

[31] See Ian Ker, 'Newman and the Mediterranean', in Michael Cotsell, ed., *English Literature and the Wider World Vol. 3 1830–1876: Creditable Warriors* (London and Atlantic Highlands, NJ: The Ashfield Press, 1990), 67–81
[32] For the following discussion see Ker, *Newman on Being a Christian*, 79–83.
[33] *Diff.* ii. 89.
[34] *Ess.* ii. 53–4.
[35] *Ess.* i. 313, 333–4; ii. 53.
[36] *LD* xx. 465.

the Catholic Church than in a Protestant church, for 'a Protestant world cannot commit that sin which a Catholic world can'. When ordinary human weaknesses are 'coupled with that intense absolute faith which Catholics have, and Protestants have not', one finds 'acts of inconsistency, of superstition, violence etc which are not to be looked for external to the Catholic Church'.[37] In other words, on the principle that the corruption of the best is the worst, if the claims of the Catholic Church are anything to go by, one would expect to find in her the greatest scandals. In particular, in regard to the papacy, 'where you have power, you will have the abuse of power – and the more absolute, the stronger, the more sacred the power, the greater and more certain will be its abuse'.[38] Because, too, the Church is a very visible polity in the world at large, it is also 'necessarily a political power, and to touch politics is to touch pitch'.[39] As in the 19th century, so in the 20th century Catholicism continues often to scandalise people in exactly the same ways.

Towards the end of his life, in the great 1877 Preface to the *Via Media,* Newman tackled the sensitive problem of corruption in a more profoundly theological manner. The Church, he points out, is the mystical body of Christ, who 'is Prophet, Priest, and King; and after His pattern, and in human measure, Holy Church has a triple office too; not the Prophetical alone and in isolation . . . but three offices, which are indivisible, though diverse, viz. teaching, rule, and sacred ministry.' It follows that Christianity 'is at once a philosophy, a political power, and a religious rite: as a religion, it is Holy; as a philosophy, it is Apostolic; as a political power, it is imperial, that is, One and Catholic. As a religion, its special centre of action is pastor and flock; as a philosophy, the Schools; as a rule, the Papacy and its Curia.' These three different offices are based on different principles, use different means, and are liable to different corruptions:

> Truth is the guiding principle of theology and theological inquiries; devotion and edification, of worship; and of government, expedience. The instrument of theology is reasoning; of worship, our emotional nature; of rule, command and coercion. Further, in

[37] *LD* xxvii. 139.
[38] *LD* xxv. 203–4.
[39] *LD* xxvii. 265.

man as he is, reasoning tends to rationalism; devotion to superstition and enthusiasm; and power to ambition and tyranny.

The difficulty of combining together all three offices is well illustrated by the question, 'What line of conduct, except on the long, the very long run, is it once edifying, expedient, and true?' Certainly, the charism of infallibility protects the Catholic Church from error not only directly in teaching but also 'indirectly' in 'worship and political action also'. However, 'nothing but the gift of impeccability granted to her authorities would secure them from all liability to mistake in their conduct, policy, words and decisions'. The problem of exercising these three very different functions 'supplies the staple of those energetic charges and vivid pictures of the inconsistency, double-dealing, and deceit of the Church of Rome'.

Far from blaming the corruptions to be found in the Church on Catholic theology, as he had once done as an Anglican, he now observes that 'ambition, craft, cruelty, and superstition are not commonly the characteristic of theologians', whereas the alleged corruptions in fact 'bear on their face the marks of having a popular or a political origin', and 'theology, so far from encouraging them, has restrained and corrected such extravagances as have been committed, through human infirmity, in the exercise of the regal and sacerdotal powers'. Indeed, religion is never 'in greater trouble than when, in consequence of national or international troubles, the Schools of theology have been broken up and ceased to be'. He then gives the reason for this in an important passage already quoted:

> I say, then, Theology is the fundamental and regulating principle of the whole Church system. It is commensurate with Revelation, and Revelation is the initial and essential idea of Christianity. It is the subject-matter, the formal cause, the expression, of the Prophetical Office, and, as being such, has created both the Regal Office and the Sacerdotal. And it has in a certain sense a power of jurisdiction over those offices, as being its own creations, theologians being ever in request and in employment in keeping within bounds both the political and popular elements in the Church's constitution, – elements which are far more congenial than itself to the human mind, are far more liable to excess and corruption . . .[40]

[40] *VM* i. xl-xliii, xlvii-xlviii.

A charge often levelled at the Catholic Church is that of the corruption of its worship, in other words of superstition. But Newman argues that the kind of popular religion likely to cause scandal may be traced to the gospel itself, and he cites the example of the woman with the haemorrhage who hoped to be cured by touching the cloak of Jesus, who 'passed over the superstitious act' and healed her because of her faith. In fact, he praised her for 'what might, not without reason, be called an idolatrous act'. Actually, the gospels show that the 'idolatry of ignorance' is not regarded on a level with other idolatries (of wealth, for example), which, however, are not normally 'shocking to educated minds'. Jesus constantly insisted on the necessity of faith – 'but where does He insist on the danger of superstition?' However, the fact remains that this and other incidents in the gospels 'form an aspect of Apostolic Christianity very different from that presented' by the Epistles of St. Paul. Newman's penetrating question, then, is: 'Need men wait for the Medieval Church in order to make their complaint that the theology of Christianity does not accord with its religious manifestations?' Does 'a poor Neapolitan crone, who chatters to the crucifix', do anything inherently more superstitious than the woman with the haemorrhage? Given 'the ethical intelligence of the world at large', Newman wonders 'whether that nation really had the faith, which is free in all its ranks and classes from all kinds and degrees of what is commonly considered superstition'.

There is therefore no need to be surprised if the Catholic Church, in the face of popular religion, finds it difficult 'to make her Sacerdotal office keep step with her Prophetical'. This applies particularly to the cult of the angels and saints, which, 'though ever to be watched with jealousy by theologians, because of human infirmity and pervaseness . . . has a normal place in revealed Religion'. For monotheism implies beings who are inferior to God but superior to human beings, and who are able to bridge 'the vast gulf which separates Him from man'. And so polytheism is only 'a natural sentiment corrupted'. The Church's mission consequently is not 'to oppose herself to impulses' that are 'both natural and legitimate', though previously 'the instruments of sin, but to do her best, by a right use, to moderate and purify them'. The fact that the Church has not always been successful simply shows that 'there will ever be a marked contrariety between the professions of her theology and the ways and doings of a Catholic country'.[41]

In conclusion, then, the two principal objections that Newman had made as an Anglican against the Roman Catholic Church, far from being removed, became paradoxically the two major arguments in favour of the Church. Instead of doctrinal developments being seen as accretions, they are now viewed as the essential growth of a living body. Similarly, corruptions in the life of the Church are no longer interpreted in a negative but a positive light: for they are now perceived as the inevitable abuses of a Church which possesses the vitality of Christianity in its fullness and in all the complexity of life itself. In short, both original arguments against Roman Catholicism, doctrinal development and practical corruption, become in effect authentic notes of the true Church – that is to say, of the *real* not the ideal Church.

---

[41] *VM* i. lxvi-lxxi, lxxiv.

7

The Fullness Of Christianity

By 1843 Newman saw that not only was the principle of doctrinal development a persuasive hypothesis to account for the facts of Christian history, but also 'a remarkable philosophical phenomenon, giving a character to the whole course of Christian thought', particularly of course to Catholic thought, lending it 'a unity and individuality' such that 'modern Rome was in truth ancient Antioch, Alexandria, and Constantinople, just as a mathematical curve has its own law and expression'. However, there was another consideration, and that was the application of the principle of development to the personal religious development of the individual, that is to say, 'the concatenation of argument by which the mind ascends from its first to its final religious idea'. Thus Newman concluded, as he put it in a key passage in the *Apologia*:

> I came to the conclusion that there was no medium, in true philosophy, between Atheism and Catholicity, and that a perfectly consistent mind, under those circumstances in which it finds itself here below, must embrace either the one or the other. And I hold this still: I am a Catholic by virtue of my believing in a God . . .[1]

As the American theologian Avery Dulles has pointed out, this 'double principle is perhaps Newman's most seminal contribution to ecumenical theology', for 'the formula challenged Catholics to acknowledge the salutary value of the faith of non-Catholic Christians and motivated Catholics to help those other Christians to deepen their own faith rather than renounce it'.[2]

---

[1] *Apo.* 179–80.
[2] Avery Dulles, SJ, 'Newman, Conversion, and Ecumenism', *Theological Studies*, 51 (1990), 725.

The principle is to be found in Newman's other Catholic writings. Thus, in *Discourses to Mixed Congregations,* he preached that

> when once a man has a real hold of the great doctrine that there is a God, in its true meaning and bearings, then (provided there be no disturbing cause, no peculiarities in his circumstances, involuntary ignorance, or the like), he will be led on without an effort, as by a natural continuation of that belief, to believe also in the Catholic Church as God's Messenger or Prophet, dismissing as worthless the objections which are adducible against the latter truth, as he dismisses objections adducible against the former. And I consider, on the other hand, that when a man does not believe in the Church, then (the same accidental impediments being put aside as before), there is nothing in reason to keep him from doubting the being of a God.

Just as belief, then, leads to fuller belief so too unbelief is characterised, at least in principle, by the same kind of progression, or rather decline: 'Unlearn Catholicism, and you open the way to your becoming Protestant, Unitarian, Deist, Pantheist, Sceptic, in a dreadful, but inevitable succession . . .'[3]

The argument is developed in the *Grammar of Assent,* where Newman posits the case of three Protestants, one of whom becomes a Catholic, another a Unitarian, and the third an unbeliever. How is one to account for such religious changes? Newman looks immediately to the explanation from development:

> The first becomes a Catholic, because he assented, as a Protestant, to the doctrine of our Lord's divinity, with a real assent and a genuine conviction, and because this certitude, taking possession of his mind, led him on to welcome the Catholic doctrines of the Real Presence and of the Theotocos, till his Protestantism fell off from him, and he submitted himself to the Church. The second became a Unitarian, because, proceeding on the principle that Scripture was the rule of faith and that a man's private judgment was its rule of interpretation, and finding that the doctrine of the Nicene and Athanasian Creeds did not follow by logical necessity from the text of

[3] *Mix.* 260–1, 282.

Scripture . . . nothing was left for him but to profess what he considered primitive Christianity, and to become a Humanitarian. The third gradually subsided into infidelity, because he started with the Protestant dogma . . . that a priesthood was a corruption of the simplicity of the Gospel. First, then, he would protest against the sacrifice of the Mass; next he gave up baptismal regeneration, and the sacramental principle; then he asked himself whether dogmas were not a restraint on Christian liberty as well as sacraments; then came the question, what after all was the use of teachers of religion? why should any one stand between him and his Maker? After a time it struck him, that this obvious question had to be answered by the Apostles, as well as by the Anglican clergy; so he came to the conclusion that the true and only revelation of God to man is that which is written on the heart. This did for a time, and he remained a Deist. But then it occurred to him that this inward moral law was there within the breast, whether there was a God or not, and that it was a roundabout way of enforcing that law, to say that it came from God, and simply unnecessary, considering it carried with it its own sacred and sovereign authority, as our feelings instinctively testified; and when he turned to look at the physical world around him, he really did not see what scientific proof there was there of the Being of God at all, and it seemed to him as if all things would go on quite as well as at present, without that hypothesis as with it; so he dropped it, and became [an] Atheist.

Newman gives another example, this time of a convert to Catholicism who returns to Protestantism, 'because he has never believed in the Church's infallibility; in her doctrinal truth he has believed, but in her infallibility, no.' How could this be? The case, as Newman diagnoses it, is by no means purely fanciful.

He was asked, before he was received, whether he held all that the Church taught, he replied he did; but he understood the question to mean, whether he held those particular doctrines 'which at that time the Church in matter of fact formally taught', whereas it really meant 'whatever the Church then or at any future time should teach'. Thus, he never had the indispensable and elementary faith of a Catholic, and was simply no subject for reception into the fold of the Church.[4]

[4] *GA* 160–2.

Of course, Newman was only too well aware that human beings are not altogether consistent, so that the kind of development he describes does not in fact by any means always take place: certain premises, which in turn depend upon certain first principles, do not necessarily lead in practice to the conclusions to which they ought logically to lead. But logically (in an informal sense) there is 'a certain ethical character, one and the same, a system of first principles, sentiments, and tastes, a mode of viewing the question and of arguing . . . which would lead the mind by an infallible succession from the rejection of atheism to theism, and from theism to Christianity, and from Christianity to Evangelical Religion, and from these to Catholicity'.[5]

As we have seen, what Newman is describing in theory actually took place in his own life, at least in his development from Bible Christianity to Catholicism. It remains to consider in what ways, if Catholicism is the fullness of Christianity, the Catholic Church herself must contain all the positive elements of the various less-than-full varieties of Christianity, which the individual believer, far from rejecting, adds to by developing their further implications. We have already seen that Newman thought the Catholic Church in his own time should herself change in order to attract converts. Since the actual historical Church, as the Second Vatican Council teaches, is always, humanly speaking, in need of reform, there may always be ways in which she can benefit and learn from other Christian communities, even though they lack the fullness of the Christian faith.[6] In the light of Newman's own experience, then, and of his critiques of the different varieties of Christianity, what kind of contribution do today's non-Catholic traditions have still to offer to the more perfect realisation of the fullness of Christianity to be found in the unity of the Catholic Church? In what ways and to what extent has the Second Vatican Council fulfilled Newman's hopes for a renewal of Catholicism? Are there new problems in the contemporary Church which that Council did not adequately address? Clearly the reforms and teachings of

[5] *GA* 321.
[6] *Lumen Gentium* 8; *Unitatis Redintegratio* 4.

Vatican II, which after all was intended to be a Council particularly concerned with Christian reunion, overlap with the kind of positive elements in non-Catholic Christianity which the post-Tridentine Church had neglected or obscured. So I shall first summarise the ways in which Newman anticipated the theology of Vatican II, before turning to the present post-conciliar period.

Newman[7] has often been called the 'Father of the Second Vatican Council'. It is true that according to the late Bishop B. C. Butler, his direct influence on the proceedings of the Council was not 'deep or determinative'.[8] And yet he was undoubtedly a great pioneering figure towering in the background, of whom the principal theologians at Vatican II were very well aware. There is certainly no doubt that Vatican II upheld and vindicated those controversial positions which he espoused in his own time and so often at his own personal cost.

First and most important is the dogmatic constitution on the Church, *Lumen Gentium,* the corner-stone of Vatican II. It was the absence of the wider ecclesiological context in which the doctrine of the papacy needed to be placed that Newman had deplored at the time of the First Vatican Council. As he argued then, the definition of papal infallibility had not come in the right 'order – it would have come to us very differently, if those preliminaries about the Church's power had first been passed, which . . . were intended'. He had hoped that the Council – which broke up, as a result of the invasion of Rome by Garibaldi's troops – would reassemble and 'occupy itself in other points' which would 'have the effect of qualifying and guarding the dogma' of papal infallibility. This was not to be, but, unlike those who supposed that the definition would render future Councils superfluous, Newman remained serenely confident that far from being the last Council, Vatican I would be completed and modified by a future Council, as had happened before in the

[7] See Ian Ker, 'Newman and the Postconciliar Church', in Stanley L. Jaki (ed.), *Newman Today* (San Francisco: Ignatius Press, 1989), 121–41.

[8] B. C. Butler, 'Newman and the Second Vatican Council', in John Coulson and A. M. Allchin (eds.), *The Rediscovery of Newman: An Oxford Symposium* (London: Steed and Ward, 1967), 245. Cit. by Nicholas Lash, 'Newman Since Vatican II', in Ker and Hill (eds.), *Newman After a Hundred Years,* 449.

history of the Church. Indeed, the history of the early Church showed how 'the Church moved on to the perfect truth by various successive declarations, alternately in contrary directions, and thus perfecting, completing, supplying each other'. The definition of papal infallibility needed not so much to be 'undone, as to be completed'. Faced with the exaggerations of the extreme Ultramontanes, he advised: 'Let us be patient, let us have faith, and a new Pope, and a re-assembled Council may trim the boat.'[9] The prophecy would take nearly a hundred years to be fulfilled, but fulfilled it was in the magnificently comprehensive teaching of *Lumen Gentium* which reaffirmed the doctrine of papal infallibility, but this time explained the primacy of the pope as the headship of the whole college of bishops.

Newman had remarked at the time of the First Vatican Council that the definition of papal infallibility would result in 'an alteration of the *elementary constitution* of the Church', because it would encourage the pope to act alone without the bishops.[10] It was 'the gravest innovation possible', for 'it is a change in the hitherto recognised basis of the Church'.[11] The phenomenon of so-called 'creeping infallibility' that occurred between the two Councils would have been no surprise to Newman.

The constitution begins not with a description of the hierarchical structure of the Church but by defining the Church as a mystery before describing it in terms of the whole People of God. This new emphasis was, of course, picked up in the new insistence on the role of the laity. Newman's own constant concern as a Catholic with the failure of the hierarchy to take proper account of the lay people who constitute easily the largest part of the Church is well summed up in the famous remark to his own bishop that 'the Church would look foolish without them'.[12] (The separate decree on the apostolate of the laity would have been especially welcome to him.) Finally, the chapter in *Lumen Gentium* devoted to the Blessed Virgin Mary can be said

[9] *LD* xxv. 278, 310.
[10] *LD* xxiv. 377–8.
[11] *LD* xxv. 100.
[12] *LD* xix. 140.

to vindicate fully the balanced Mariology of Newman's *Letter to Pusey*, which, in its close adherence to Scripture and the Fathers, is also a pioneering example of ecumenical theology at its best.

Newman supported early ecumenical initiatives as an Anglican, and later as a Catholic he hoped for a reconciliation of Anglo-Catholics with Rome, which he thought should be prepared to make concessions. As in general in theological matters, he was cautious but open: he did not see his way to joining the 'Association of the Promotion of the Unity of Christendom', but he deplored its harsh condemnation by the Roman authorities; unlike some enthusiastic Catholic ecumenists, he was highly sceptical about the foreseeable possibility of the reunion of Canterbury and Rome, but he deplored the bigotry of so many Catholics who, he felt, considerably underestimated the possibility of 'invincible ignorance' among non-Catholics. Again, the radical statement that 'all other truths and acts of religion are included' in repentance and faith in Christ,[13] must be balanced against Newman's inability to accept that the Church of England was a church at all; he would have been surprised, albeit pleasantly so, by the degree of ecclesial reality that the decree on ecumenism attributes to the Christian bodies that derive from the Reformation. Nevertheless there was no doubting his commitment to the first faint stirrings of the ecumenical movement; and he was pleased by the successful sales of a new edition of his *Parochial and Plain Sermons* among Protestants: 'Whatever tends to create a unity of heart between men of different communions, lays the ground for advances towards a restoration of that visible unity, the absence of which among Christians is so great a triumph, and so great an advantage to the enemies of the Cross.'[14]

There are three other major conciliar documents which Newman also anticipated. The dogmatic constitution on Revelation insists on the intimate connection of Scripture and tradition, refusing to endorse the post-Tridentine 'two sources' theory. As an Anglican, Newman had assumed the inseparability

[13] *LD* xx. 172.
[14] *LD* xxiv. 22.

of Scripture and tradition, and later as a Catholic he held that
the disagreement on this point between Anglicans and Catholics
is a purely verbal one, since Scripture requires tradition for its
interpretation and tradition needs the authority of Scripture.
The constitution's teaching that the inspiration of Scripture
extends only to 'that truth which God wanted put into the
sacred writings for the sake of our salvation'[15] vindicates
Newman's own tentative approach in the article he wrote in the
last years of his life 'On the Inspiration of Scripture' (1884).

The possibility of religious truth outside the Christian
revelation is explicitly allowed for not in this constitution but in
the decrees on non-Christian religions and on the Church's
missionary activity. Newman himself in his first book had boldly
affirmed, 'There never was a time when God had not spoken to
man', for although it was true that 'the Church of God ever has
had, and the rest of mankind never have had, authoritative
documents of truth, and appointed channels of communication
with Him', still 'all men have had more or less the guidance of
Tradition, in addition to those internal notions of right and
wrong which the Spirit has put into the heart of each
individual'. Calling this 'vague and uncertain family of religious
truths, originally from God ... the *Dispensation of Paganism*',
Newman came to what was then the radical conclusion that the
Christian apologist or missionary should, 'after St. Paul's
manner, seek some points in the existing superstitions as the
basis of his own instructions, instead of indiscriminately
condemning and discarding the whole assemblage of heathen
opinions and practices', thus 'recovering and purifying, rather
than reversing the essential principles of their belief'.[16]

The pastoral constitution on the Church in the modern
world, *Gaudium et Spes,* encouraged exactly that creative and
positive engagement with the secular world that Newman so
vainly desiderated in his own time, and particularly with those
intellectual problems raised by scientific progress and
secularisation. Newman has often been criticised for his lack of
involvement in pressing contemporary social questions; he

---

[15] *Dei Verbum II.*
[16] *Ari.* 80–1, 84.

himself noted at the end of his life, 'It has never been my line to take up political or social questions, unless they come close to me as matters of personal duty.'[17] But there was one political idea, quite radical then, which he embraced from the beginning of the Oxford Movement and to which he continued to adhere as a Catholic – with, it should be said, much greater hope of its practical realisation: I refer to his conviction that the Church, as in the first centuries, must once again become a *popular* Church, a Church of the people. I think that there can be no question that the emergence of the Church as a popular institution in countries like the Philippines and in Latin America would have delighted Newman. Deeply shocked as he was by what he called the 'great scandal' of Pius IX being 'protected against his own people by foreign bayonets',[18] Newman surely would have rejoiced at the sight of John Paul II personally upholding the rights of the poor and oppressed in so many Third World countries. Long before it happened, Newman had seen that the establishment of Catholicism was not only anachronistic but also in practice ultimately harmful to the interests of the Church. The disengagement or distancing of the Church from the state in so many Catholic countries since the end of the Second Vatican Council Newman would have seen as inevitable and in the long term thoroughly beneficial. In 1864 he wrote:

> I am not at all sure that it would not be better for the Catholic religion every where, if it had no very different status from that which it has in England. There is so much corruption, so much deadness, so much hypocrisy, so much infidelity, when a dogmatic faith is imposed on a nation by law, that I like freedom better. I think Italy will be more religious, that is, there will be more true religion in it, when the Church has to fight for its supremacy, than when that supremacy depends on the provisions of courts, and police . . .

He also saw very clearly that the refusal to grant religious freedom to non-Catholics in Catholic countries, however justifiable (as it then seemed) on the abstract ground of the truth of the Catholic religion, was utterly impractical and self-

---

[17] *LD* xxx. 209.
[18] *LD* xxv. 217.

defeating in a modern, pluralist world. Catholicism had to be defended 'by reason, not by force'.[19] The declaration, in fact, on religious freedom would have been seen by him not only as a useful practical measure but also as an example of the development of doctrine, called for by the times.

After that brief survey of the ways in which Newman anticipated the teachings of Vatican II, it is time to consider how the different varieties of Christianity that contributed to his own personal religious development may still have positive elements which can help contemporary Catholicism reveal more manifestly the fullness of Christianity. It is perhaps not surprising that the most attention will be given to Evangelicalism, which is clearly the most vibrant form of Christianity today, apart from Catholicism to which it presents a very serious challenge, not only on the practical level in certain parts of the world (particularly Latin America), but also in terms of its methods of evangelism.

We have seen how Newman's own theology and spirituality were first formed by his deep knowledge of the Scriptures, and he would of course have greatly welcomed the post-conciliar emphasis on the Bible, although this did not, as earlier noted, mean that Church and tradition are in any way superseded or can be dispensed with. Moreover, Newman condemned as leading to heresay a merely 'literal and critical' interpretation that ignores what he called the 'mystical' or 'allegorical' sense.[20] But apart from this kind of Biblicism so characteristic of contemporary Catholic Biblical exegesis and theology, Newman would be highly critical of the selective and unbalanced approach of much modern Catholic spirituality towards the Scriptures. The actual selection of texts often shows a marked indifference to the wholeness of Scripture and the need to keep a balance between the different emphases. This one-sidedness is reinforced by, and in turn encourages, a secularising interpretation, in which the tenor and tone of the Biblical passages in question are made to reflect the priorities and values of a latent liberal humanism.

[19] *LD* xx. 477.
[20] *Ari.* 404–5

A Christian spirituality really steeped in Scripture will, in particular, maintain a balance between crucifixion and resurrection, and therefore between sorrow and joy. If pre-Vatican II Catholicism tended to be gloomy and guilt-laden, it could certainly be argued that the pendulum has now swung too far the other way. As an Anglican, Newman preached that 'we must fear and be in sorrow, before we can rejoice. The Gospel must be a burden before it comforts and brings us peace.'[21] Without severity, love itself will be a sentimental counterfeit: 'I wish I saw any prospect of this element of zeal and holy sternness springing up among us, to temper and give character to the languid, unmeaning benevolence which we misname Christian love.' To speak only of God's love and never of his just wrath is spiritually debilitating. Instead, Newman urges, it is necessary to 'condense' one's 'feelings by a secure discipline' and to be 'loving in the midst of firmness, strictness, and holiness'.[22] Unfortunately, people 'find a difficulty in conceiving how Christians can have ... sorrow and pain without gloom ... how they can believe that in one sense they are in the light of God's countenance, and that in another sense they have forfeited it'.[23] Given the fallen state of human nature, Newman has no doubt that what tends to be the neglected side of Christianity needs particularly emphasis – so much so that he is even prepared to say that those 'who seem only to fear, or to have very little joy in religion ... are in a more hopeful state than those who only joy and do not fear at all' – although, admittedly, the latter 'are not altogether in a right state'.[24]

As a Catholic, he did not feel the same need to stress the severe side of the gospel. But while he would have rejoiced at a contemporary Catholicism which has recovered a sense of the resurrection and of pentecost, he would lament that such a gain should be at the expense of a spirituality of the cross. A true Scripture-based faith is instead 'always sorrowing' with Christ in his death, 'while it rejoices' in his resurrection.[25] This explains

[21] *PS* i. 24.
[22] *PS* ii. 286, 289–90.
[23] *PS* iv. 121.
[24] *PS* iv. 134.
[25] *PS* iv. 324 .

why 'none rejoice in Easter-tide less than those who have not grieved in Lent'. For it is our own 'previous humiliation' which 'sobers our joy' and 'alone secures it to us'.[26] Again, it is the 'duty of fearing' that 'does but perfect our joy; that joy alone is true Christian joy, which is informed and quickened by fear, and made thereby sober and reverent'. The 'paradox' of combining two such opposite emotions is only really 'fulfilled in the case of men of advanced holiness'.[27] For such a union of contradictory feelings can only arise out of a deep sense of the mystery of redemption:

> Christ's going to the Father is at once a source of sorrow, because it involves His absence; and of joy, because it involves His presence. And out of the doctrine of His resurrection and ascension, spring those Christian paradoxes, often spoken of in Scripture, that we are sorrowing, yet always rejoicing; as having nothing, yet possessing all things.[28]

Another instance of the same kind of imbalance is the current obsession in popular Catholic spirituality with self-affirmation, itself a reaction against an excessively condemnatory and guilt-centred spirituality. It is true, of course, that Jesus, for example, teaches that we must love our enemies as we love ourselves; but he also tells us that we must hate our own life, lose our life in order to save it – an admonition which does not seem to be properly reflected in a spirituality of self-fulfilment. Not that such imbalances are wholly due to reactions against imbalances on the other side: there is always the spirit of the age to be taken into account. It was clear to Newman that the 'world' always 'chooses some one or other peculiarity of the Gospel as the badge of its particular fashion for the time being'. The hallmark of the modern world is its concern for human rights and social justice: 'There is a steady regard for the rights of individuals . . . for the interest of the poorer classes.' Highly commendable in itself, there is always, however, the danger of any special emphasis producing an imbalance: what his time lacked, Newman thought, was 'firmness, manliness, godly severity'. Of

[26] *PS* iv. 337–8.
[27] *PS* v. 66–7.
[28] *PS* vi. 121.

course he was to find, as a Catholic, only too much firmness, insensitivity, and severity in the church of his adoption. Perhaps, though, he might find in the 'caring' post-Vatican II Church the same kind of deficiency as he had complained about as an Anglican in the philanthropic religious culture of Victorian England. The perennial problem for the Christian, he said, is 'the reconciling in our conduct opposite virtues', whereas it is comparatively easy 'to cultivate single virtues' like compassion.[29] The antidote lay in knowing the New Testament, not selectively, but as a whole in all its spiritual dimensions, with the cross and the resurrection as the two polar points of reference. Newman's complaint as an Anglican that Evangelicals both misused Scripture as a teaching authority and quoted selectively and misleadingly from the Biblical texts is a charge that can be levelled against certain contemporary Catholic teachers. The answer for Newman was not to downplay Scripture, since it was precisely a closer and deeper understanding of the Bible that revealed both the importance in the New Testament of Church as well as tradition and also the gospel of Christ in all its various aspects and fullness.

It is time to look at the kind of challenge that the rise of Evangelicalism in parts of the world presents to the post-conciliar Catholic Church. Evangelical Christianity is likely to continue as the only vital and growing form of Protestantism, since the closing of the Counter-Reformation at the Second Vatican Council poses a very serious question to all those churches born out of the protest of the Reformers against the Catholicism of the 16th century. The fact that the Catholic Church in the 20th century has now recognised and conceded so many of the legitimate complaints of Protestantism inevitably raises a question mark over the justifications of Christians to continue in separation from the Church presided over by the successor of St. Peter, the senior Apostle. An Evangelical may reasonably claim that only that type of Protestantism which has remained faithful to the fundamental tenets of the Reformation concerning justification by faith alone and Scripture as the sole teaching authority deserves to remain in existence.

[29] *PS* ii. 279–80, 282.

Evangelicalism challenges Catholicism in two different parts of the world in two different ways. First, it has been making serious inroads into the more cultic than practised religion of Latin America where sects from the United States preaching an extremely narrow and fundamentalist version of Evangelicalism have drawn away millions of barely instructed, nominal Catholics. The explanation for this phenomenal development in recent years largely lies in the desperate political and social conditions in many parts of the sub-continent, which on the one hand offer fertile ground for a revivalist kind of Christianity (with many material inducements on offer) and on the other hand have understandably led the Catholic Church to concentrate on issues of justice and peace at the expense of other aspects of the gospel. Secondly, it is this same failure to evangelise that has, at least in English-speaking countries, given the widespread impression that only Evangelicals are seriously interested in converting people to Christianity. Even allowing for the obvious retort that Catholics cannot participate in the kind of proselytising activities favoured by militant Evangelicals, it is still arguable that the pre-conciliar apologetics designed to prove that the Catholic Church was the true Church have hardly been replaced in any very effective way by a serious commitment to preaching the fullness of the Christian faith to a society increasingly more pagan than Protestant. A particular problem, indeed, lies in the very area of preaching homilies: Evangelicals have never been hesitant about delivering lengthy sermons which of course concentrate heavily on the atonement and justification by faith; whereas, although the homily is now seen as an integral part of the eucharist, Catholic priests, directed by Vatican II's constitution on the liturgy to draw their inspiration from the Scripture readings, have tended not to include much doctrinal teaching in their liturgical preaching, which often degenerates into mere moralising. Here Newman's example as an Anglican preacher could be a wonderful stimulus, for in those classic sermons preached at St. Mary's, Oxford we find an extraordinarily powerful fusion of the doctrinal, liturgical, moral, and spiritual, all within the framework of a reflection on a text from Scripture.

It seems to be true that while Vatican II gave the Church in missionary countries, such as in Africa, a new freedom from alien cultural forms so that she could preach the gospel more effectively, in W. Europe and N. America the effect of the Council was rather the opposite as ecclesiastical energy was consumed in ecumenism, social action, and in the reform of internal church structures. It was Pope Paul VI's *Evangelii Nuntiandi* (1974) that marked a new beginning, but a serious realisation of the need for a Catholic re-evangelisation of the West has been slow to mature. In English-speaking countries the Catholic Church's traditional role of defending and promoting Catholicism against Protestantism was replaced after the Council by a flurry of intense, often naively optimistic, sometimes irresponsible ecumenism, which has now slowed down in the face of a more realistic awareness. But the realisation that the Catholic Church, now the largest practising Christian church, in Britain, the United States, and the older Commonwealth countries, has now the primary responsibility for preaching the fullness of the Gospel in the face of the increasingly vocal voice of a narrow Evangelicalism is only just beginning to dawn.

The fastest-growing Evangelicalism is now to be found where there is in fact a strong ecclesial dimension in the restricted sense of a cohesive local community. Where this is combined with charismatic worship, as in the so-called Community Church, we find the fastest-growing variety of Christianity, in Britain at any rate. It is true that the post-conciliar Catholic Church has made great efforts to build up a sense of community, but all too often this has not been combined with a similar energy in preaching the gospel, or with a sufficient understanding that the Church is a community only because of the presence of the Holy Spirit. In other words, a supernatural conception of the Church has all too often been replaced by an excessively social understanding.

An evangelical body like the Community Church naturally equates the 'church' with the local congregation. But, while the post-conciliar Catholic Church has laid great stress on the role of the laity, this has tended to be regarded by the hierarchy and clergy in too clerical a light. Many lay people have welcomed this because they see the issue as primarily one of power within the institution. However, a glance at the teaching of Vatican II on the people of God shows how superficial this approach is. In fact, the real understanding of the true Christian *power* of the baptised that Newman in his own time possessed and that the French theologian Yves Congar developed in his classic study *Lay People in the Church: A study for a Theology of the Laity* (English tr. 1957), has come not from the episcopally-inspired committees of the official Church, but rather from those lay people who constitute the rapidly growing lay movements and communities that are the most striking, and surely the most hopeful phenomenon in the contemporary Church. It is to this remarkable development that we must look to find an adequate Catholic response to the Evangelical discovery of 'people power'.

The Catholic charismatic renewal movement, for example, has led to the growth of new communities of varying degrees of commitment to the full religious life, ranging from families living in close proximity to each other to celibate male and female community houses. Charismatic renewal has also stimulated new evangelistic initiatives in the United States, especially among college students, while in France it has produced many of the vocations to the priesthood as well as recent nominations to the episcopate. Again, the fast-growing Italian lay movement, Communione e Liberazione, which has now spread to other countries, is particularly strong among university students and presents a Catholic counterpart to the Evangelical Christian Union in British universities or the Crusade for Christ on U.S. campuses The fact that some of the new (or not so new) lay movements are highly controversial should not surprise us: it was the same with older religious orders and communities. Criticism partly arises out of suspicion of whatever if unfamiliar, but also partly is no doubt sometimes provoked by excessive or misguided zeal. However, it is worth noting that the movements vary from the uncontroversial Focolare movement to the equally controversial Communione e Liberazione. Some of these basically lay movements, such as the Neo-Catechumenate, are now ordaining priests for the movement.

Newman's own theology of the laity has regularly been trivialised in terms of the kind of 'consultation' that is characteristic of secular institutions concerned with the exercise of power. This is not to say that Newman was not well aware of the importance of this kind of human power in the Church, which, as we have seen, he realised very clearly was undeniably an institution from one point of view. He had after all himself written in the original passage in the *Rambler* which had begun the controversy, that the Catholic bishops should 'really desire to know the opinion of the laity on subjects in which the laity are especially concerned'.[30] But, as we have seen, there was also a much deeper sense in which Newman thought the bishops must consult the lay people, and that is because they *are*, largely speaking, the Church. What is so interesting to realise in retrospect is how Newman anticipated the rise of the 20th century lay movements, which many observers see today as the contemporary equivalent of the early monks or the medieval friars or the Jesuits of the Counter-Reformation, in both renewing the Church herself and in evangelising the world.[31]

The fact is that Newman's thinking about the laity began in the very early stages of the Oxford Movement, when he wondered whether the time had not come for the Church of England, threatened by state interference from a reforming parliament, to become what he called a 'popular' church. After all, he pointed out, the 'early Church threw itself on the *people*'. His own first public act as a Tractarian was to write the first of a series of articles 'called the "Church of the Fathers" ... on the principle of popularity as an element of Church power'.[32] It looked as if political pressures would dictate such a change, but 'what may become necessary in time to come, is a more religious state of things also', and in practice 'the Church, when purest and most powerful, *has* depended for its influence on its consideration with the many',[33] being 'in most ages ... based on a popular power'.[34] Indeed, the Western Church 'rose to power, not by the favour of princes, but of people', and, although it was not 'developed upon its original idea' of 'appealing to the people', still 'what we do see from the first ... is, religion throwing itself upon the people'.[35] Even after the definition of papal infallibility when Ultramontane authoritarianism and

[30] Cit. in *LD* xix. 129.
[31] See Paul Joseph Cordes, *Charisms and New Evangelisations*, Eng. trans. (Middlegreen, Slough; St. Paul Publications, 1992).
[32] *LD* iv. 14, 18.
[33] *HS* i. 341–2.
[34] *LD* iv. 35.
[35] *Ess.* i. 150–1.

clericalism were at their peak, Newman was still hopeful that 'the Catholic Church may at length come out unexpectedly as a popular power'.[36] At least the papacy, however, was no longer encumbered with the papal states, and Newman looked forward to the disestablishment of the Church in Catholic countries where the imposition of the faith by law was becoming increasingly counter-productive. The Church could only be effective to the extent that it was really constituted by the people.

Not only did Newman want a popular Church; he also anticipated the modern phenomenon of the lay movement. He was after all the leader of the Oxford or Tractarian Movement, and initiated the *Tracts for the Times* that he insisted should be written by individuals, not least by laymen, and distributed by personal contacts – 'Living movements do not come of committees.'[37] Literary as well as theological propaganda was needed, and Newman encouraged his friend Maria Giberne and his sister-in-law Anne Mozley to write 'Apostolical stories' for children.[38] When he looked back at such prominent precursors of the Movement as Alexander Knox, the Irish theologian, and the poet Coleridge, he was struck by the fact that they were both 'laymen and this is very remarkable', as was Dr. Johnson, 'another striking instance'.[39] Many of the leading members of the Movement were lay, including prominent public figures like Gladstone.

When the Roman Catholic hierarchy was restored to England in 1850, storm of anti-Popery erupted in the face of this so-called 'Papal Aggression'. Newman's response to the publicly orchestrated campaign against Catholics is very interesting. He thought it could be profitably exploited by making it an excuse for 'getting up a great organisation, going round the towns giving lectures, or making speeches, . . . starting a paper, a review etc.' He recommended gathering laymen to speak at public meetings in the big towns. Young Catholics particularly, he felt, should band together as the Tractarians had. In other words he

[36] *LD* xxv. 442.
[37] *Apo.* 46.
[38] *LD* v. 387.
[39] *LD* v. 27.

saw the possibility of another 'movement', although this time he seems to have seen it as much more lay than clerical. He seems to have sensed that here was the potential beginning of another movement like Tractarianism, the occasion being again the persecution of the Church, although this time a different Church. But he was disgusted that the Catholic bishops had not bothered nor did they intend to consult the laity on the best course of action to take. His own bishop, he was convinced, 'has a terror of laymen, and I am sure they may be made in this day the strength of the Church'.[40]

Newman himself embarked on a series of public lectures in June 1851, which were intended to counteract the traditional English prejudice against Catholicism. They were published in book form as *Lectures on the Present Position of Catholics in England: Addressed to the Brothers of the Oratory.* These 'Brothers of the Oratory' constituted the so-called 'Little Oratory', which was the confraternity of laymen traditionally attached to an Oratory. Of all the Oratorian activities and works, Newman considered this as 'more important than anything else'.[41] The Oratory, after all, had started in Rome as a kind of lay community led by St. Philip Neri, the so-called 'Apostle of Rome'. It had not been intended to be another congregation or order of priests. The first 'Oratory' was simply the group of laymen that gathered for discussion and prayer and study with St. Philip. Full community life came later when an inner or 'core' group began to live together, three of whose members were ordained to the priesthood. We can see from Newman's surviving Oratory papers[42] that he was very conscious of the original lay basis of what eventually developed into the Congregation of the Oratory, in which the few lay members would be subordinated to the priestly majority. In recognising the 'Little Oratory' as indispensably attached to the Oratory, Newman was consciously or unconsciously adverting to the Oratory's essentially lay antecedents. Not content with the traditional 'Little Oratory' of laymen, Newman in 1856 proposed

[40] *LD* xiv. 214, 252.
[41] *LD* xiv. 274.
[42] *NO.*

to the Pope 'the formation of a female [little] Oratory'.[43] Of
course a 'Little Oratory' only consisted of a relatively small
number of lay people closely associated with the local Oratory.
But when we take into account Newman's hope that the Oratory
would spread through the cities and towns in England, we can
see how such an extended 'Little Oratory' would in fact have
formed a kind of widespread lay movement, although it would
be as loosely knit as would the individual autonomous Oratories.
Needless to say, Newman's dream was never fulfilled.

Turning to the third of our varieties of Christianity, we do not
need to say more of the dangers posed by the liberal spirit to the
contemporary Catholic Church. If an anti-dogmatic liberalism is
always a temptation to the fallen human mind which seeks to
make itself the judge of all things, then the Church is bound to
be especially prey to it in a time of confusion after a Council. As
for Newman's liberal Catholicism, all that needs to be said here
is that his attempt to maintain a balance between the demands
of the magisterium and those of theologians affords us today a
valuable example of a truly authentic comprehensiveness. At a
time when Catholics are wont to take up either conservative or
liberal positions, it is well to remind ourselves that it is possible
to do justice to both sides without loss of integrity. One can
accept and welcome the essentially negative vigilance of Rome in
protecting discipline and doctrine, without at the same time
denying the right of theologians to explore in a critical spirit.
But just as authority must be tempered with tolerance, so
originality requires a sense of loyalty and responsibility.
Newman's approach to these vexed questions also shows how
impossible it is to lay down exact lines of demarcation between
two different principles which complement even as they oppose
each other in a potentially creative conflict.

The theology and spirituality that Newman learned from the
Greek Fathers should certainly not be out of place in the Church
of the Second Vatican Council, as they were bound to seem in
the scholastic Church of the 19th century. But when people
complain that those who speak airily of the 'spirit of Vatican II'
do not always seem particularly well acquainted with what the

---

[43] *LD* xvii. 137.

Council actually taught, essentially what they are saying is that the mystery of the Church, so splendidly evoked in *Lumen Gentium,* has been secularised and trivialised. The so-called abuses of the post-conciliar period are all part and parcel of a desacralisation which stems from a more or less secular model of the church. And this in turn is no doubt at least partly the result of a low christology which stresses the humanity of Christ as much as an older Catholicism emphasised his divinity, with the same disastrous result that the two natures of Christ become separated in a way that, as we have seen, the East has always avoided. There is no doubt that the distortions of the Council's teachings would have appalled Newman, but not surprised him particularly: the violent reaction against the old ossified system he predicted; but revolutions are in the habit of replacing one evil with another, often disquietingly similar, evil. If the old model of the Church had its roots in a feudal, hierarchical society, the new model often seems to owe more to the sociology of an egalitarian society than to the New Testament or the Fathers – or Vatican II. Not surprisingly, the cut-and-dried abstractions of a scholasticism which often seem to have lost touch with Scripture, the Fathers, and St. Thomas Aquinas himself, and the rigidities of Roman juridicalism, have all too often been replaced by horizontalism, neologism, and the casual permissiveness of a pluralist society. Thus in the liturgy, which expresses so concretely our understanding of the nature of the Church, mechanical formalism has been replaced by a studied (but no less clerical) informality, and legalistic rubricism by popular gimmicks. Similarly, the sacraments, no longer viewed as conveying automatic 'packets' of grace (itself seen as an abstract quality of the soul), are now often practically reduced to the level of community 'celebrations'. A consumer culture has little interest in the past, so history and tradition are neglected in today's Church, for example in the scant attention paid to the saints, with an impoverishing effect on spirituality. A materialistic, welfare society has as little time for sin, as it has for suffering, and so in today's Church penance is minimised, while a popular psychology confuses repentance with guilt. At the same time a culture which values so highly what it calls self-fulfilment cannot tolerate the sacrifice involved in the ideal of

virginity (so often again admittedly impoverished in the old pre-
Vatican II Church by negative and purely pragmatic
considerations).

The right response to all these and other distortions and
misunderstandings is not to attempt to retreat into the pre-
conciliar Church but to recover a vision of that mystery of the
Spirit-filled Church that we find in the New Testament, the
Fathers, Newman, and Vatican II. One obvious reason why this
has not happened is that so many of the leaders of the Church,
who were educated in the old manual theology, understandably
threw away their manuals in the 1960s, and are now virtually
without any real theology at all. The Catholic charismatic
renewal began in the United States as a reaction against the
secularism of the immediate post-conciliar period. It was a sign
of the times: a sign not that everybody should become
'charismatics' but that the Church must once again start
believing in the third person of the Trinity, the person, as we
have seen, that the East has never neglected or confused with the
other persons. But the Holy Spirit is not the spirit of the times,
as liberal Catholics sometimes seem to imply. Newman's
Anglican writings on the Holy Spirit provide a magnificent
inspiration for a renewed theology of the Church, which would
remedy so many of the defects of contemporary Catholicism and
correct so many distortions of the Second Vatican Council. To
see the Church sacramentally as the communion of believers
baptised in the Spirit is to avoid the trap of viewing the Church
in terms of a secular model of society. To understand the
sacraments in the light of the same Spirit who alone makes them
possible is to ensure that they are seen as essentially personal
encounters with the living Christ, and as conveying grace
because in them God gives us the gift of himself through his Son
Jesus Christ and by the power of the Holy Spirit. To appreciate
the profound implications of the divinisation of the flesh by the
Spirit, which is the incarnation, is to avoid that pervasive
contemporary gnosticism which has seeped into the Catholic
Church and so stresses the spiritual at the expense of the fleshly
that even the virginal conception and the bodily resurrection are
now being doubted by some Catholic teachers, for whom they
have ceased to have any real significance for faith.

It is the contention of this book that Newman, through his appropriation of the positive elements and through his criticism of the negative elements in the main varieties of Christianity, offers not only a unique approach to the fullness of Christianity in Catholicism, but also an invaluable critique of the present state of the Catholic Church.

Index

147